passes that comfort on to her readers. Mothers are especially on her heart, but anyone will be blessed and helped in the troubles they face as they take in Christine's wisdom and receive her compassionate care.
—**Lauren Whitman**, Faculty and Counselor, CCEF

*Midnight Mercies* is a compassionate and valuable resource for those who are navigating the depths of depression, darkness, and related shadowy struggles. Christine Chappell's personal understanding and compassion shine through as she offers meaningful guidance for how to respond to these struggles in ways that magnify God's grace. *Midnight Mercies* is a beacon of hope and help for anyone who longs for solace amid the shadows of depression.
—**Rush Witt**, Lead Pastor, Paramount Church, Bexley, Ohio; Author, *I Want to Escape*

For the mama who feels mired in inescapable despair and defeat, Christine provides a gospel-saturated path toward hope and wholeness. She powerfully silences the whisper that you're alone in your depression or mental diagnosis by vulnerably sharing her own story and then walking through the narratives of some of Scripture's most faithful who experienced their own dark valleys. What a gift and help *Midnight Mercies* will be to so many!
—**Lisa Appelo**, Author, *Life Can Be Good Again*

Christine's insights teach us much about God's compassion and how we can trust him with our lament as well as come alongside others who are experiencing an emotional midnight. Immediately after I read *Midnight Mercies,* a hopeless friend asked for help and I felt ready to walk with her with Christine's book in my hands. I highly recommend it.
—**Sharon W. Betters**, Author, *Treasures in Darkness*; Executive Director, MARKINC Ministries

Vulnerable, honest, and abundantly hopeful, Chappell unflinchingly confronts some of the hardest realities of living in a fallen world and unfailingly points to our assurance in Christ.
—**Kathryn Butler**, Author, *Glimmers of Grace*

*Midnight Mercies* ministers not only to mothers who are walking through dark nights of the soul but to any woman who has been stricken with deep grief and pain. Christine candidly shares her own experiences while also working through the stories of biblical sufferers such as Moses, Elijah, Mary and Martha, Job, Naomi, and others. It is a must-read for all who have experienced brokenness and need practical encouragement to hold onto the hope we have in Christ.
—**Camille Cates**, Speaker; Biblical Counselor; Author, *Moving Forward after Abortion*

This book offers tremendous hope by providing unique and nuanced counsel that digs deep into the various emotions involved in depression. A varied readership will find relatable, extensive help in a very readable format.
—**Dave and Krista Dunham**, Counselors, Sparrow and Heart Soul Care; Authors, *Table for Two*

*Midnight Mercies* is a rare book that interweaves the sharing of painful suffering, vulnerable personal stories, and tender faith in God. Though Christine writes to mothers who face depression, leading them by the hand through her own experience, the wisdom in *Midnight Mercies* will connect with sufferers of many types.
—**Ellen Mary Dykas**, Director, Equipping for Ministry to Women, Harvest USA; Author, *Jesus and Your Unwanted Journey*

If you feel weighed down by the sorrows of motherhood, you're not alone. Humbly sharing her own story and honestly confronting the questions we all face, Christine Chappell is both a sympathetic friend and wise counselor. In her thoughtfully written book, Chappell reminds us that while our pain is real, so is our hope, and we can trust the God who walks with us. I highly recommend *Midnight Mercies*!
—**Katie Faris**, Author, *God Is Still Good*

Christine Chappell comes alongside the hurting with biblical hope. Readers won't find trite responses or false self-rescue advice; rather, Christine gives voice to the reality of depression and the merciful God who enters the pit with us and offers us rest in him. If your heart is hurting today, read *Midnight Mercies*.
—**Christina Fox**, Counselor; Speaker; Author, *A Heart Set Free*

*Midnight Mercies* invites you to a rare pairing: an author who is willing to bring you into her darkest hours but who expresses her pain in the language of healing theology. Chappell doesn't shy away from

the hardest problems or the hardest Scriptures, yet she manages to find insightful encouragement in Christ again and again. I commend this honest, uplifting work to anyone, especially struggling mothers.
—**Alasdair Groves**, Executive Director, Christian Counseling & Educational Foundation (CCEF); Coauthor, *Untangling Emotions*

In this excellent book, Christine Chappell shows us the heart of a mother who is struggling with depression. She has given us many useful insights, including a definition of the difference between normal sadness that is safe and sadness that puts a struggling mother at risk. Knowing the difference can be lifesaving.
—**Charles Hodges**, Executive Director, Vision of Hope Residential Counseling Facility for Women

Christine's vulnerable testimony points not only to the reality that we all struggle in a broken world but also to the truth that throughout all time God has been at work in the lives of those he calls his own. May his love and care minister to your soul as you take in Christine's humble story of suffering.
—**Jonathan D. Holmes**, Executive Director, Fieldstone Counseling

Christine shares how depression affected her as a mother, shedding light on the underlying issues that can lead to depression and giving hope in Christ to other suffering mothers.
—**Shannon Kay McCoy**, Biblical Counseling Director, Valley Center Community Church; Council Member, Biblical Counseling Coalition

Christine does a wonderful job of weaving her personal story with the experiences of God's people in Scripture. She compassionately offers struggling moms hope in the gospel.
—**Jim Newheiser**, Executive Director, The Institute for Biblical Counseling and Discipleship

*Midnight Mercies* is a must-read for moms who are struggling with depression, and I plan to buy extra copies to give away. Christine is my go-to person on issues of mental health, and her wise counsel, biblical examples, and firsthand experience make this book so helpful. As she vulnerably shares her journey of depression, Christine reminds readers that they are not alone in their struggle and that God will unfailingly meet us when we feel forsaken.
—**Vaneetha Risner**, Author, *Desperate for Hope* and *Walking through Fire*

Christine knows depression is bleak. She is also confident that God has been her steady companion through it. She tells pieces of her story that will help you to learn to trust God's loving presence in your depression too. Her advice is kind. Every passage of Scripture Christine shares is relevant to types of suffering that depression brings.
—**Jenny Solomon**, Speaker; Cofounder, Solomon SoulCare; Author, *Reclaim Your Marriage*

Overflowing with hope and grace, this book is a treasure chest of helpful transparency and biblical wisdom for any woman who is walking through a dark valley.
—**Paul Tautges**, Pastor; Counselor; Author, *Anxiety*

*Midnight Mercies* is a sweet gift for the weak and weary. Walk with Christine as she speaks personally and tenderly about the desolation of depression and our God who meets us in seasons of sorrow. God has gifted Christine with comforting scriptural insights, which she captures so well they will be anchors for your soul when you desperately need his mercies.
—**Darby A. Strickland**, Counselor, CCEF; Author, *Is It Abuse?*

The Lord has comforted Christine in her troubles and, with both refreshing transparency and keen biblical insights, Christine now

# MIDNIGHT MERCIES

# MIDNIGHT MERCIES

*Walking with God through Depression in Motherhood*

CHRISTINE M. CHAPPELL

P.O. BOX 817 • PHILLIPSBURG • NEW JERSEY 08865-0817

Italics within Scripture quotations indicate emphasis added.

Appendix A first appeared on *Risen Motherhood* as "When Grief Becomes Dangerous (and What to Do about It)," April 17, 2023, https://www.risenmotherhood.com/articles/when-grief-becomes-dangerous-and-what-to-do-about-it. It has been adapted for this book.

*Cover design by Jelena Mirkovic*

ISBN: 978-1-62995-884-2 (pbk)
ISBN: 978-1-62995-885-9 (ePub)

Printed in the United States of America

Library of Congress Cataloging-in-Publication Data has been applied for.

For my mother, Diane, and my husband, Brett

The darkness never could manage to separate
me from God's faithful love,
nor from yours.

# CONTENTS

# FOREWORD

"Some days, it feels so hard to breathe. Other days, I just wish my breath would stop coming."

I sat across from my husband, trying to piece together words that might at least scratch the surface of my inner turmoil. But it was clear—as much as he wanted to understand, we were speaking different languages and looking at the world through completely different lenses. While my world was painted in black and white, his was painted in color. While mine was filled with distortions, his was filled with clarity. While mine was covered in clouds, his was illuminated by the sunlight. Deep down, I was convinced that no one would ever be able to truly enter into the dark void that left me feeling like a stranger to myself, a burden to others, and a faithless Christian. The light of hope seemed to have vanished.

*Hope*—it can seem like such a distant and empty word at times, can't it? This dark and disorienting pit of depression can leave us floundering, lost, detached, and ashamed. And as moms, we carry the guilt of knowing it doesn't only affect us—it affects those we love the most: our children.

If this is where you find yourself now or where you've found yourself in the past, you are *not* alone—despite how lonely it feels. The dark night of depression can taunt us with accusations and doubts, whispering in our ear that *good* Christians don't despair and, *if we just had more faith*, then the light of hope would break through the darkness that surrounds us. But the truth is, there is far more to the story, and that hope we long for is not so much dependent on how much we *feel* its presence or see it in our circumstances, but in Someone outside of ourselves—the person of Jesus.

So, from one who has endured many *midnight* seasons to another, my hope and prayer is that you will not only feel seen and heard on the pages of this book, but that you will come to find Christine's honest, real, and compassionate words to be a balm to your heart, soul, and mind, as they have to mine. Not because she has all the answers, but because she has been there—where depression has threatened to consume and define her—and yet has found the treasures of Christ's comfort, nearness, and grace in her own dark night of the soul to be sufficient—even precious.

The hard but beautiful truth is that although these midnight hours may come with a vengeance, leave us disoriented, and often seem to have no end in sight, the sun shining again is not where our true hope and strength is found. As Christine so beautifully shares, our hope and strength is found in the light and presence of Jesus, not in the absence of darkness.

Although depression has been a frequent and unwanted visitor in my life, I have experienced the preciousness of walking with my Savior and seeing firsthand that he will never let me go—no matter how dark things may appear. By God's grace, these midnight seasons no longer define me and they certainly haven't been wasted. Yes, they have been immensely painful, but God has also redeemed them—shaping me in a way that has kept me tethered to him. And for that, I wouldn't want it any other way.

One day, my friend, the darkness will lift and the sun will shine again—either in our lifetime or the next—but until then, you and I can be assured of this: when midnight comes, his mercies will meet us there.

Sarah Walton<br>
Coauthor, *Hope When It Hurts*

*Introduction*

# STARTING OUR JOURNEY

What did you expect when you found yourself expecting?

Years ago, I imagined motherhood would be full of joyous milestones and memorable moments. What I didn't expect was so much hurt, heartbreak, conflict, and disappointment. I've often felt clueless and incapable. I've beaten myself up for not being the mother I thought I *should* be—the kind of Christian woman who can handle whatever comes her way with pep in her step and a smile on her face. That's one of the reasons that I wrote this book. I wanted to debunk the notion that faithful believers never groan as they wearily plod through the miserable muck of life. God knows they do. Frequently.

Although much of what I share in these pages is relevant to suffering saints in general, I offer *Midnight Mercies* specifically to depressed mothers because there are so few biblical resources that give voice to their experiences of despair. Suicide attempts among pregnant and postpartum women are a real and pressing issue. That "mommy needs wine" to cope with stress and sorrow has become a highly marketable and socially acceptable message in the United States—even among professing Christians.[1] As a mother whose story includes suicidal ideations and alcohol use in depression, I want to bear witness to Christ's light in the dark night of the soul.

Depression is no respecter of persons—moms of all ages and stages can find themselves walking through a season of unexpected and lingering misery. So if you're a Christian mother whose world has gone dark, and you feel guilty or ashamed that you can't figure out how to turn the lights back on again, I pray that the Lord will use this book to lift that burden off your back. Let's not focus on how you think you "should" be feeling right now. Instead, let's start by giving voice to the hurt in your heart.

Maybe today it feels like you're being forced to bear up under the impossible. Maybe you feel so utterly burdened beyond your strength that you despair of life itself. Or maybe you just feel sad and disheartened by the trouble and disappointments you've faced as of late. It's okay to admit where you are right now. It's much more helpful to be honest than to pretend that life isn't hard for you today. The sorrow, pain, and confusion you're going through *are* hard—you *are* suffering.

Maybe your groans sound like these:

I'm misunderstood and mishandled by others.
If only I was different, I'd be worthy of love.
If God was good, I wouldn't be suffering.
I'm a failure and a burden to my family.
No matter what I do, nothing changes.
I feel like I'm praying to a brick wall.
I feel unwanted, unseen, and unclean.
My sorrow has swallowed me whole.
My life has no meaning or purpose.
I should be doing better than this.
I've forgotten what happiness is.
I can't live like this anymore.
I must not be saved after all.
Life will never be different.
God is disappointed in me.

I'm at the end of my rope.
I've ruined everything.
The future is bleak.
There's no hope.

I know *I've* groaned each one of these statements before. Sometimes silently with a stiff upper lip. Other times with red cheeks and a roar of rage.

Although you too may identify with some (or all) of these statements, what can be harder to identify are the emotions that underwrite them. You may look at these words and conclude, "I'm depressed"—and that's not an incorrect phrase to describe how you're feeling. But the word *depression* is a term that encapsulates a multifaceted human experience. This means that much more could be said to describe what it feels like to be you today. Maybe you're feeling hopeless, or weary, or sad. Maybe you're angry, or anxious, or ashamed. Maybe you're feeling lonely or some muddled combination of the entire lot.

Because depression skews our perception and interpretation of reality, it can be difficult for us to see ourselves rightly or describe our experiences accurately. But with God's help, acknowledged emotions can become more manageable emotions. Thus, I'd like to help you to connect your groans to someone who went through a similar experience and consider if their groans reveal something meaningful about your own. I'll do this by sharing my own story, as well as composite characters based on real people and their real experiences that give us glimpses into the lives of mothers in the throes of despondency. More important, I'll focus on unpacking biblical narratives that provide a big-picture view of how God mercifully engages desperate people. By selecting key stories—ones that depict raw and relatable moments of human distress—I hope to bring you comfort for your journey and counsel for your next steps.

As you read the stories that follow, you may be tempted to think you have it easier than those who are walking through "more severe" suffering. But I want to caution you against this comparison trap. Just because it could be worse for you doesn't mean it isn't hard for you. And what's hard for you specifically—be it a trial, trouble, or temptation—is a real affliction that has God's focused attention. If it burdens your spirit, it burdens him. Because Jesus loves you and cares about the war waging within you, don't discount the difficulty of your problems by comparing them to someone else's (1 Peter 5:7).

You'll see that I often make summary statements—just like the one in the paragraph above—that reference specific Scripture verses or passages. I encourage you to look up these parenthetical references. If it's too cumbersome to search for them as you read, consider revisiting them as fuel for personal devotions.

Sister, there are no new problems under the sun. Although no two experiences of depression are exactly alike, despondency is a distinctly *human* problem. Though the path through this darkness is daunting, it's also well-traveled. Generations past have made it *through*, and *out*, and, by the grace of God, *up*. It's true. The "huge cloud of witnesses" (Heb. 12:1) includes despondent believers who made it through the dark, and out of the dark, and up from the dark *alive*. The light of life came to them in time. And by God's midnight mercies, it will come to you too.

You're going to make it. You'll see.

And I will lead the blind<br>
  in a way that they do not know,<br>
in paths that they have not known<br>
  I will guide them.<br>
I will turn the darkness before them into light,<br>
  the rough places into level ground.<br>
These are the things I do,<br>
  and I do not forsake them. (Isa. 42:16 ESV)

# 1

# HOPELESSNESS

## *A Dangerous Fire*

After weeks of languishing, I told my husband what he already suspected: I was in urgent need of help. I can't remember if we took a picture of her or not—all I know is that our daughter's first day of sixth grade was also the first of my seven days in the psychiatric hospital. After she got on the bus, I packed a small bag and got into the car, uncertain when I would see her again. Acting on the advice of our insurance provider, my husband and I drove to the emergency room for an immediate evaluation.

This wasn't the first time I'd been hospitalized for self-harm and suicidal thinking, but it *was* the first time I limped through those double doors as a believer in Christ.[1] And as much as I'd like to say my faith was a comfort, my Christian identity seemed only to compound my shame. After all, why would I want to die if I'd been raised to new life in Jesus? Why did it seem like God had abandoned me after he'd promised he wouldn't? Where was he? Why was he silent? And why, after all my trying—after all my Bible reading and praying and studying and memorizing and repenting and serving—hadn't I better learned how to sail the seas of sorrow when they stirred?

The only answer I could see at the time? The Holy Spirit must have packed up and left me.

When this darkest of midnights fell, I was thirty-four years old, a married mother of three at the end of her rope. The months leading into this season of darkness had taken our family through a cross-country move on a shoestring budget. Our relocation meant saying goodbye to the only church family I'd ever known and saying hello to a season of overwhelming distress and uncertainty. In the midst of these major life changes and the conflicts that accompanied them, I was assailed by unprocessed griefs, festering relational wounds, and the everyday noise and chaos of raising three children. Tantrums. Arguments. Accidents. Relentless late night wake-ups. Early morning emotional blow-ups. The physical, emotional, and mental drain of it all was suffocating.

I didn't want to live like that anymore.

## PUSHED TO THE BRINK

Sometimes heavy onslaughts of grief and trouble overpower our ability to cope with everyday responsibilities. Are you feeling buried alive under your burdens? Suffocated, trapped, and desperate for escape? Hopeless? Maybe you don't know how you're going to manage the next fifteen minutes, let alone persevere through the trials God has brought you to. You may feel as though you are on the brink of a total meltdown.

Some Christians think they should never experience this kind of overwhelm. But the reality is that life is often hard to handle—even for believers (2 Cor. 1:8). We all have disordered hearts. We all engage in disordered relationships. We moms are all raising children with disordered affections in a world of disordered hope and power, and we do it in the fragility of disordered bodies—vessels originally built to last that now must die. The futility of living a hard-to-handle life in a fallen world is one reality that depression sees clearly.

## MOSES'S MELTDOWN

The Scriptures recognize the pain of our disordered reality as well. God's Word is replete with stories of real believers who really faltered under the weight of what God was calling them to do or go through. Because these raw accounts narrate the history of God's people, they're a part of your history as well; the hindsight afforded to us through them can provide deep insight in seasons of darkness. When we observe how God faithfully engaged his desperate people back then, we learn much about the means he uses to care for us now.

Numbers 11 offers a candid account of this overwhelm-in-action. Moses was a man who spoke with God face-to-face as a man speaks to his friend (Ex. 33:11). But in this passage we find him at the end of his rope. Months earlier, God had chosen him to lead the nation of Israel out of slavery, through the wilderness, and up to the promised land. But as he obeyed God's calling, he grew increasingly overwhelmed—particularly when it came to managing the needs of the people entrusted to his care. Nothing ever seemed to be enough for the wilderness wanderers. All they did was constantly complain.

One day, in a fit of hopeless desperation, Moses snapped. Frustrated and desperate for relief, Moses had what we might call a total meltdown.

> Why are you treating me, your servant, so harshly? Have mercy on me! What did I do to deserve the burden of all these people? . . . I can't carry all these people by myself! The load is far too heavy! If this is how you intend to treat me, just go ahead and kill me. Do me a favor and spare me this misery! (Num. 11:11, 14–15)

Does Moses's frankness before God surprise you? It certainly dispels the notion that "real" believers are always calm, cool, and collected in overwhelming situations. This man had spent more time in the presence of God than any mortal! They had an intimate friendship, no less! And yet Moses was just a man after all. Fully human. Fully finite. Fully capable of succumbing to hopeless desperation—just like the rest of us.

## NO ONE IS IMMUNE

Do you know what it's like to feel as Moses did that day? Like God is expecting too much from you? Like he's treating you unfairly? You're not the only believer who knows what it's like to groan, "I can't carry all these burdens by myself—they're too heavy! If this is how life's going to be for me, I quit! I can't live like this anymore!" Our desire to escape from the overwhelming aspects of life—and our tendency to despair when we can't—is an innate part of the human experience. All of us know what this is like to some degree.

And that's an important point, particularly for those of us who feel ashamed about our struggles. No born-again believer, however advanced in her spiritual maturity, is immune to buckling under life's unrelenting pressures. As Charles Spurgeon said, "This disease of soul-dejection is common to all the saints—there are none of God's people who altogether escape it."[2] Scripture makes a point of highlighting the truth that even believers at times would rather quit life than continue to slowly suffocate under the weight of their burdens.

I'm not saying this is a right response to suffering, but it's a real one. We do ourselves no favors by getting stuck on the idea that true Christians never feel like this. They do.

## OUR RESPONSE, GOD'S RESPONSE

I deeply resonate with the response we see squeezed out of Moses's overburdened heart. Under the weight of his calling, he totally lost his composure. He buckled under the incredible pressure he felt and lashed out at God as a result.[3] I've experienced total meltdowns like this, to be sure. It is discouraging when all your toil and obedience appear futile. It is defeating when nothing works the way you hoped, no matter how faithful you try to be in your God-given roles and responsibilities. And when the pressures and pains of motherhood become too burdensome to bear—when it seems like God is failing you or has fallen asleep on the job—it is natural to want to "fly far away" (Ps. 55:7), to take it upon yourself to find the relief you're looking for.[4]

But as we move through this narrative in Numbers, see how God responds to his dear friend's despair. Frankly, he wasn't accountable in any way to Moses. God didn't owe the man an explanation, nor did the accusations of Moses put him on the defensive. And yet, being quick to listen, slow to speak, and slow to anger, the Lord graciously chose to *counsel* Moses in the midst of his meltdown:

> Gather before me seventy men who are recognized as elders and leaders of Israel. Bring them to the Tabernacle to stand there with you. I will come down and talk to you there. I will take some of the Spirit that is upon you, and I will put the Spirit upon them also. They will bear the burden of the people along with you, *so you will not have to carry it alone.* (Num. 11:16–17)

God's response was not severe or merciless but rather full of "grace, understanding, and assistance."[5] He wasn't enraged by his servant's frustration and confusion; he didn't rebuke Moses for his resentful, unrighteous attitude (although he did so in a separate instance; see Num. 20:12); in the heat of the moment, he didn't lecture Moses about the bitterness bubbling up in his overburdened heart. God knew Moses's meltdown would not be corrected by an immediate spiritual dissection. Figuratively speaking, the man was on fire! *Extinguish first, investigate later.* That's wisdom.

That's mercy.

## GOD'S COUNSEL IS PERFECT

You probably know how unhelpful poorly timed counsel can be. The right words spoken at the wrong moment only add to our burden. But when God himself counsels hopeless and desperate people, the words he speaks are both well-timed and well-seasoned with grace and understanding. He's not shocked when we're shaken —"he knows how weak we are; he remembers we are only dust" (Ps. 103:14). So when his people become frustrated and confused by the weight of their circumstances, his manner toward them is neither harsh nor hasty. The Wonderful Counselor only ever says what we need to hear—what's going to be most helpful.

In this exchange, the counsel he gives to Moses is something for us all to consider, especially when it feels like we "can't do this anymore." After all, if anyone knows how to help you when you're falling apart, surely it's the One who knit you together.

## THE NECESSITY OF SUPPORT

So what was God's counsel to his despairing servant? The Lord knew Moses was overwhelmed and discouraged by his circumstances. Yet rather than offering this weary man escape or deliverance, God helped Moses by telling him to seek the support of Spirit-filled people. And when we're feeling hopelessly overwhelmed, this is often our most immediate need as well.

God brings light to our darkness through the care of other people.

I realize this counsel may sound trite or even make you feel uneasy, and I don't suggest it lightly. Some of our burdens are so private, so shrouded in stigma, or so painful that it can take time to determine whom to trust them with. Maybe you've tried asking for help before, only to be misunderstood or disappointed. To be sure, we need to exercise wisdom and discernment when looking for care and counsel. But discretion needn't keep us from seeking the support of Christian community, particularly in the context of a healthy local church whenever possible.

We don't have to immediately disclose every detail about our situations to receive the practical help and ongoing spiritual encouragement we need in this season of life. Brothers and sisters in Christ can still minister God's Word to us, sit with us, pray for us, listen to us, share a meal with us, direct us to relevant resources (such as books, support or advocacy groups, or mercy ministries), and help with chores or childcare.

Although we were designed to do life together in a local Christian community, sometimes this can be a source of pain and grief. We may crave connection with other Christians but have trouble finding it. But however discipleship and fellowship might look like for us in this dark season, we need to know that God doesn't expect us to carry our burdens alone or to navigate depression on our own. Rather, he's calling us to seek the kind of care and counsel that comes from outside ourselves. We can't do this. We haven't "got this."

We need help.

## PRIORITIES

Think of it this way: If you noticed your house was on fire, what would your first response be? Would you search the internet for videos on fire safety and prevention? Grab a piece of paper and map out a detailed evacuation plan? Curl up in a closet and wait for the flames to go out on their own? No! When my family's house caught fire a few years ago, the very first step I took was to dial 911 (while screaming for my kids to get outside). In the literal heat of the moment, my most immediate priority wasn't to determine what had caused the fire—it was to call for the help of first responders.

What *wasn't* I thinking as our roof melted down? "We shouldn't be having a fire!" or "Real Christians never have house fires!" or "If only I had prayed the right way—if only my faith was stronger—then we wouldn't be homeless right now!" House fires can happen to anybody, and the time to analyze them is not while the flames are raging.

The same holds true with hopelessness—it can happen to anybody under the "right" circumstances. So if you're having a total meltdown—if you feel overwhelmed beyond your ability to cope and want to give up—recognize first that you're a woman on fire. Sure, you may be thinking, "I shouldn't be feeling this way" or "Real Christians never feel hopeless!" or "If only I had prayed the right way—if only my faith was stronger—then I wouldn't be so depressed right now." But such thoughts only serve to stoke the fire. They don't help you to put out the flames.

*Hopelessness can quickly become dangerous—especially when we try to fight against it alone.*

Yes, there is investigative work to do when you feel hopelessly overwhelmed by life, but timing matters. Your steps forward need to be prioritized. Whereas your most urgent priority may be to seek escape or relief, sometimes the best "way out" (1 Cor. 10:13) of meltdown moments is to call out to God *and* other people for help.

Sister, God isn't asking you to toughen up, get your act together, and figure out how to manage life on your own. He's not expecting you to extinguish the raging flames of hopelessness in solitude. He knows you cannot carry these burdens by yourself and continue to function in your God-given calling. Although it's right for us to pray for mercy when we're having a total meltdown, there's another fire-quenching step we can take as well.

Call out to the nearest "first responders" you know.

## MOVING TOWARD SAFETY

The morning I disclosed the extent of my hopelessness to my husband, a new chapter in my story began. Though he couldn't deliver me from my overwhelming despair, I was no longer carrying its full weight alone. Neither of us knew exactly what kind of help I needed just then, but God used my husband as a first responder—as a means of midnight mercy to me. As he began to make phone calls on my behalf, my downward spiral slowly started to stall. In less than an hour, my next step came into focus: *go to the ER*. And although this was a step I was extremely reluctant to take, I feebly took it for Christ's sake. He had bought me with a price—I was not my own (1 Cor. 6:20).

Sister, if we saw the holy temple in Jerusalem burning to the ground, wouldn't we cry out for someone to help? "God's house is on fire! Quick! Somebody grab the water!" Hopeless desperation in depression is no different. Your body is God's temple, and you're burning (1 Cor. 6:19). Though it can be dangerous to try to fight the fire on your own, you can move toward safety through the ministry of Spirit-filled helpers—those who are wise, understanding, and experienced (Deut. 1:13; Prov. 11:14). Seeking the practical help and ongoing support of Christian community doesn't specifically address the reasons that we feel the way we do, but it's a step of first importance—an immediate priority.

Your need for help is not a character flaw—it's God's design.

Drew Hunter writes, "When we're left to ourselves, we quickly descend into the dark places of our souls. This is why we need good companions who stay with us and who empathize with us. When they join us in our downcast moments, they may not feel like they're doing much, but they're holding a candle in our darkness."[6]

God knows how quickly we descend into dark places when life feels like it's too much to bear. But he also knows that we have need of "candle holders"—those who'll support and steady us as we walk through this darkness. The journey ahead *will* be too much for you without them. A mother who stands alone in depression "can be attacked and defeated, but two can stand back-to-back and conquer" (Eccl. 4:12). Get someone's help to fight the urge to quit when you can't carry on.

## NEXT STEP

Cry out to God for mercy, then call out to someone you trust and tell them how you're feeling.

*Listen to my prayer, O God. Do not ignore my cry for help! Please listen and answer me, for I am overwhelmed by my troubles. (Ps. 55:1–2)*

## REMEMBER

When I feel hopeless and overwhelmed by life, I will remember that God doesn't expect me to suffer stoically in solitude but instead instructs me to immediately seek the fellowship, counsel, and support of Spirit-filled people.

## REFLECTIONS FOR PERSONAL APPLICATION

1. Describe how you're feeling today. Did any words or phrases in this chapter resonate with your experience?
2. Note one insight you gleaned in this chapter about your experience of hopelessness.
3. Note one step you can take today to apply what you've learned in this chapter to your own situation.
4. What have you learned today about the mercy of God toward those who feel hopeless?

# 2

# WEARINESS

## *The Feeling of Defeat*

Maybe you're reading this chapter fresh on the heels of a hopeless meltdown. Or perhaps you're feeling drained and discouraged. In depression, it's common for us to vacillate between emotional temperatures: frustrated and irritable one minute, numb and apathetic the next.

By the time I arrived at the emergency room, I mostly felt weary and desperate for emotional stability. That, and afraid of going through another psychiatric hospitalization. I'd been down that road before. But we had to do something—and apparently this was it.

Even so, walking through the hospital doors felt tantamount to surrender. After fighting so hard for so long, how had I come to be here again? I felt like a failure . . . a loser . . . an embarrassment of a Christian, wife, and mother.

Do you know what that's like? To feel completely, totally, utterly defeated?

Kay's been there too. Never in her wildest dreams had she imagined an unwanted divorce would become part of her story, but not long after she welcomed a daughter into the world, her husband welcomed another woman into his arms. The months that followed his adulterous abandonment were some of the darkest Kay had ever known. She struggled to keep pace at work. She failed to keep her appointments. And she couldn't keep from wondering what she could or should have done to keep her family from falling apart.

She felt worn down and defeated. This wasn't the story she wanted.

## WEARY AT MIDNIGHT

Motherhood is wearying by nature. But when layered trials, physical exhaustion, and a grieving spirit collide, weariness can slide into despair. This may take the form of life-disrupting apathy. Our cognitive capacities may diminish, making it difficult for us to process information and accomplish simple tasks. And as we feel "unable to do what our responsibilities demand, we are harassed by accusing and condemning thoughts regarding our every mistake and blunder, both real and imagined."[1] We become "harassed at every turn—conflicts on the outside, fears within" (2 Cor. 7:5 NIV).

This kind of weariness leaves us feeling unable to "run with endurance the race God has set before us" (Heb. 12:1). We not only lose heart but lose patience. We get tired of doing what's good because it seems to be doing no good at all (Gal. 6:9). And in those defeating moments of life, when sorrows are many and solutions are few, we don't know what to do with ourselves—what to do about *any* of it.

We throw up our hands in surrender and cry, "I can't live like this anymore!"

We simply haven't the strength. Our will is wavering.

We want a change.

## ELIJAH'S WEARY DEFEAT

In 1 Kings 19, we meet someone who knows what it's like to feel downright defeated: Elijah. With God's help, this prophet had multiplied a widow's food supply and raised her dead son back to life (17:14–15, 22). He had triumphantly called down fire from heaven and slain 450 prophets of Baal (18:37–40). Talk about an obedient servant—Elijah was a divinely empowered miracle worker! But as bold as his faith had proved just days before, in 1 Kings 19 we find him cowering in the wilderness. All it had taken to send him there was a hard day and a death threat:

> Jezebel sent this message to Elijah: "May the gods strike me and even kill me if by this time tomorrow I have not killed you just as you killed [the prophets of Baal]."
>
> Elijah was afraid and fled for his life. He went to Beersheba, a town in Judah, and he left his servant there. Then he went on alone into the wilderness, traveling all day. He sat down under a solitary broom tree and prayed that he might die. "I have had enough, LORD," he said. "Take my life, for I am no better than my ancestors who have already died." (vv. 2–4)

"I've had enough," Elijah groaned. But why? After all he had seen and done with God's help, why did he buckle like this? Why did he run from a death threat only to ask God for death? Charles Spurgeon suggests that Elijah's common sense was reeling after "such a hard day's work, such stern mental toil, such marvelous spiritual exercises."[2]

Whereas Moses faulted God, Elijah faulted *himself*. He believed that he was no better than his ancestors. He felt like a failure . . . a loser . . . an embarrassment. Alone and harassed by his thoughts, feeling unable to do what his calling required, "he admits defeat in that, in his human strength, he [has failed] . . . in keeping Israel faithful to the Lord."[3]

## NOT SUPERHUMAN

Once again, we observe that even the mightiest of God's servants can slip into hopeless desperation. And sometimes that slip comes by way of their weariness. Though God would later honor Elijah like none other by carrying him "by a whirlwind into heaven" (2 Kings 2:11), even the great Elijah knew what it was to "go down to the pit . . . like one without strength" (Ps. 88:4 NIV).[4] He knew what it was for his will to waver.

Although Elijah was called to a ministry of supernatural deeds, he wasn't superhuman. And if this midnight has taught us anything so far, it's that neither are we. Mothers may not be called to work miracles of Old Testament proportions, but we are called to the kind of ministry that requires great expenditures of our resources and energy.

Are you struggling to "be highly capable and energetic in child-rearing"?[5] If so, it doesn't mean you're a failure, a loser, or an embarrassment of a Christian mother. Rather, it means you're human and you need help—just like the rest of us. Contrary to popular messages from our twenty-first-century Western culture, to be human is to be intrinsically finite and needy. There's no such thing as self-made flourishing (1 Cor. 4:7). All of us depend on the provision and help we receive from God and others. This reality is easily forgotten when we feel highly capable and energetic and sorely remembered when we feel weary and desperate for an outcome that we cannot accomplish on our own.

> We're all reaching for that elusive gold star: becoming the women society says we can be. We keep pulling ourselves up by our bootstraps, guzzling our coffee, and looking in the mirror to remind ourselves, "You got this, sister. Go get 'em." But then. *Then.* Almost without exception and as if on cue, we reach the end of ourselves. The coffee cup is empty. The self-talk grows

> quiet. We collapse on the couch. We are tired. This isn't working. Someone send help.[6]

"I got this!" is the cry of a supermom, but "Help!" is the cry of a saint who knows her need.

## SICK AND TIRED

Yet Elijah didn't cry out for help. He was groaning to quit. He was ready to give up the good fight. From his blurred perspective, the race God set before him was one of failure and futility. Because he wasn't seeing the kingdom fruit he thought his obedience would produce, he lost both heart and patience. His body was tired, and his spirit was sick (Prov. 18:14). He couldn't pull himself together.

If Elijah was not immune to deep discouragement, we can safely assume that it's normal for us to experience it as well. Do you feel (1) physically drained, (2) unable to do what your responsibilities demand, (3) incapable of producing the outcomes you desire, and (4) beaten down by accusing and condemning thoughts? If you've answered yes to all these questions, you know what this kind of discouraging weariness feels like. To borrow the words of civil rights leader Fannie Lou Hamer, you may well be feeling "sick and tired of being sick and tired."[7]

Is it a wonder, then, that the moments we feel most sick and tired are the moments we most feel like giving up? Yes, we want our circumstances to change—and that's not necessarily wrong! But when circumstantial change becomes a prerequisite for our perseverance—when immediate deliverance seems more appealing than courageous dependence on Jesus[8]—hope becomes deferred and makes our heart sick (Prov. 13:12). It feels futile to carry on.

Weariness can lead us to shift our hope from Christ to change.

## "SHOW ME HOW TO LIVE!"

Joni Eareckson Tada knows what it's like to feel weary and depressed. On July 30, 1967, she broke her neck in a diving accident. In an instant, the seventeen-year-old went from being a highly capable athlete to a fully dependent quadriplegic. In the weeks that followed, she often prayed to die in order to escape her misery, but God refused her desperate requests time and time again.

All she wanted was death, but the Lord kept giving her life.

One day, Joni "was so sick and tired of the despair and the feelings of self-pity, [that she] cried out, 'God, if I can't die, *show me how to live.*'" This desperate cry of faith was life-changing for her: "The next morning I woke up a different person."[9]

I can't promise that changing your groans from "Lord, I've had enough!" to "Lord, show me how to live!" will help you to wake up a different person tomorrow. But it's worth noting that God responded to Elijah as if he'd groaned that way—as if the weary prophet had asked for the strength and faith he needed to run the race set before him with endurance.

When we are feeling depressed and defeated, it's "not up to us to ask for death but for life."[10]

## WHAT ELIJAH NEEDED MOST

What we next observe in this scene is endearing. It's reminiscent of a parent caring for a sick child—one who doesn't have the sense to know what he needs or the strength to get out of bed.

> Then [Elijah] lay down and slept under the broom tree. But as he was sleeping, an angel touched him and told him, "Get up and eat!" He looked around and there beside his head was some bread baked on hot stones and a jar of water! So he ate and drank and lay down again.

> Then the angel of the LORD came again and touched him and said, "Get up and eat some more, or the journey ahead will be too much for you."
>
> So he got up and ate and drank, and the food gave him enough strength to travel forty days and forty nights to Mount Sinai, the mountain of God. (1 Kings 19:5–8)

Notice what the angel *didn't* say to Elijah as he lay faint under the tree. We don't hear phrases like "You got this, Elijah. Go get 'em!" or "Repent of your self-pity, Elijah! The world doesn't revolve around you!" It makes me wonder what I would have said to him in that moment. Would *I* have offered Elijah a pep talk or rebuke?

We learn a lot about God's heart for the weary as we observe his patient care for Elijah. The Wonderful Counselor knew his servant was in no condition to do much of anything, let alone participate in a sensible conversation. He also knew that Elijah's collapse was related to his earnest desire to serve his Lord. Yes, his perceived lack of success had disheartened Elijah to the point of despair.[11] But he had exhausted every ounce of himself in an effort to be faithful to his calling, and God knew it (Heb. 6:10).

It's encouraging to see (yet again) that the Lord approaches hopeless and desperate saints *mercifully*. Elijah hadn't a clue about the help he needed right then. He couldn't pick himself up out of the pit—he didn't even try! But God knew exactly how to sustain his servant for service, and he used that special knowledge to revive Elijah's will.

## GOD SHOWS US HOW TO LIVE

Though we do well to prioritize bodily care as we're able in this season, that's not the main reason I brought us to this story. My goal is to help you to see God's mercy for those who feel defeated and desperate. Our Father doesn't kick his children when they're down—and Elijah's story shows us that.

Now, was this eat-drink-sleep routine the only step Elijah needed to take in addressing his hopelessness and the weariness that fed it? No. But did the Lord consider Elijah's physical refreshment to be irrelevant or unimportant to the spiritual conversations to come? No. Before God addressed Elijah's despondent soul directly—before he asked any heart-probing questions—God patiently addressed his servant's wilted condition. Once again we see that the Father's response is full of grace, understanding, and assistance.

Inviting Elijah to partake of basic, life-sustaining necessities was God's first priority. It was also something his weary servant could immediately act on. All that was required of Elijah in his moment of despair was to (1) sit up and (2) eat and drink. Elijah obliged, then lay back down to sleep. He had done what God had given him to do.

God refused Elijah's request to die. Then he showed him how to live.

I also want to highlight Elijah's response to the Lord's care. Namely, that he was willing to accept the miraculous yet ordinary provisions God offered to him. Why do you think that was? He said he wanted to die, so why agree to take nourishment? Could it be because the man knew his life was not his own (1 Cor. 6:20)? Because he viewed the angel's touch, the food, and the water as God's way of comforting and strengthening him? Courageous dependence looks like this sometimes—viewing life-sustaining basics as a means of God's help.

As a heavenly nudge to keep pressing on.

## TAKE ONE FEEBLE STEP OF FAITH

Never in my wildest dreams did I think that reclining on a gurney in the psychiatric corner of the ER would be God's way of showing me how to live. But that one hard day, with the threat of death hanging over me, it was. After seeking the counsel of a number of others, we realized that going to the ER was the clear step the Lord had put before us. And I think that says a lot about God's merciful manner with us as we walk through depression. Just like we saw with Elijah and Moses, God reveals the steps of our journey to us at a pace he knows we can manage: one by one. Yes, he will ask heart-probing questions along the way, but he gets there in good and perfect time.[12]

God will not grow weary of your need for help, nor will he ever tire of being your strength (Isa. 40:28–31).

Elijah's story also speaks to the merciless manner in which we're tempted to view our shortcomings. We often kick ourselves when we're down. We often task ourselves with accomplishing outcomes that God hasn't required of or promised to us. We often begrudge our weaknesses and limitations, not only viewing them as consequences of the curse but curses themselves. They seem to prove that we really are nothing more than failures . . . losers . . . embarrassments.

But although our weariness may amplify the condemning clamor in our thoughts, it does no such thing in the thoughts of God. He doesn't think less of us when we're sick and tired; he doesn't help us less when we're hopeless and desperate. Rather, he bears with the weary in mercy and cares for the needy in love.

God knows when we're beating ourselves up—it's not in him to add to the punches.

Sister, if it seems like this journey is too much for you today, that's because it is (1 Kings 19:7). And God's goal for us on days like this is not that we would rise to the occasion like self-sufficient supermoms but that we would rely on him like suffering saints who know their need. He says, "Come to me," not "Go get 'em!"; "Take my rest," not "Rally time!" (Matt. 11:28). If all you can manage to do right now is take one faithful, feeble step in the strength God supplies, that's not at all defeat but great success. You're learning how to live when all you want to do is quit.

That's no small victory. That's faith in action.

## NEXT STEP

Pray for God to show you how to live in the strength he supplies today.

*Don't be afraid, for I am with you. Don't be discouraged, for I am your God. I will strengthen you and help you. I will hold you up with my victorious right hand. (Isa. 41:10)*

## REMEMBER

When I feel weary of the hardships in my life and nothing I do seems to make a difference, I will rest in the fact that God has not called me to accomplish an outcome but to take my next feeble step of faith in obedience to him.

## REFLECTIONS FOR PERSONAL APPLICATION

1. Describe how you're feeling today. Did any words or phrases in this chapter resonate with your experience?
2. Note one insight you gleaned in this chapter about your experience of weariness.
3. Note one step you can take today to apply what you've learned in this chapter to your own situation.
4. What have you learned today about the mercy of God toward those who feel weary?

3

# SADNESS

## *Facing the Unfixable*

I'll never forget the sadness I felt after signing the voluntary admission papers. I wept. My face grew hot. Looking through the one-way window of the psychiatric wing, I saw my husband collapse into tears. Never had I seen him so broken. Never had I felt so broken. Though separated by a thick pane of security glass, our hearts were united in grief over a problem we didn't know how to fix.

If today you feel swallowed by sadness over a problem you don't know how to fix, you're not the only one.

Two months after the death of Abby's mother, Abby's fourteen-year-old stepson was diagnosed with an autoimmune disorder. After nine months of watching her mom wither away, Abby spent eight months shuttling Brandon from doctor to doctor. Nothing seemed to help his pain—at least, not for long. And try as they might to present a united front, Abby and her husband often argued late into the night over their son's care and their family's financial burdens. They'd never known such powerlessness before. It was overwhelming.

Some days, Abby drowned her sorrows in wine. Other days, she drowned herself in DIY projects. Most days, tears were just one shouting match away from flooding her tired eyes. All the prayers her dying mother had mumbled for a miracle that never came, all their crying out and pleading to God for their boy's broken body to heal—and nothing. Nothing. All Abby could do was watch life break before her eyes. Her mother's death and son's disease were not only heartbreaking but humanly unfixable.

## A FRONT-ROW SEAT TO SUFFERING

Not all who feel swallowed by sadness have recently met death face-to-face. But we all know what it's like to grieve over the brokenness we experience and witness. Disease. Disorder. Disunity. All is not right, and all creation is groaning. Although some may view death and disease as only natural, they're not original to this world. God didn't make us to break us. Human sin is to blame for wrecking what God created to flourish.

Now pain and loss are a part of everyday life. Even motherhood often boasts as many or more sorrows as it does joys because the curse has spoiled every good gift the Father gives. The sadness we rightly feel about this spoiling—about having a front-row seat to a parade of decay—is an "honest assessment of and reaction to"[1] this hard-to-handle life.

Not only do we experience and witness brokenness on a daily basis, but, most devastatingly, sometimes there's nothing we can do about it. In 2011, I watched my dad slowly succumb to cancer. The grief I felt as I witnessed his suffering was compounded by the fact that I could do nothing to stop it. I could not take away his pain. This is the harsh reality of the broken world we live in.

Such helplessness can leave us feeling hopeless.

## OBEDIENCE AND FAITH DON'T GUARANTEE HAPPY OUTCOMES

As we saw in the previous chapter, Elijah was grieved (in part) by the nation of Israel's disobedience. His sorrow was compounded by the fact that he was powerless to turn the people's hearts back to God. Helpless to accomplish his desired outcome and feeling like a failure, he ignored his many successes and downplayed the value of his faithful obedience. As weariness consumed him, he became desperate and hopeless. But even though Elijah wasn't thinking straight or seeing reality clearly in the thick of his despair,[2] God was merciful in focusing his prophet's immediate attention back to ordinary, life-sustaining basics.

Faithful obedience belongs to us. Final outcomes belong to God.

Though we may wonder how it will be possible for us to endure this season of sorrow, our Father already knows how he will sustain us through it. That the Lord is faithful to order our steps is surely a comforting reality (Ps. 37:23)! But it may also be a perplexing one because those steps don't guarantee that we'll get the outcomes we hope for. And when God's mysterious ways allow heartbreaking and humanly unfixable problems to enter our lives, we may find ourselves asking hard questions, like the one we find in John 11: "[Jesus] healed a blind man. Couldn't he have kept Lazarus from dying?" (v. 37).

## MARY AND MARTHA'S STORY OF GRIEF

Couldn't Jesus have done something to prevent the death of Lazarus? In John 11, we find two sisters in mourning and an entire community wondering why Jesus hadn't come to the rescue. A few days prior, Mary and Martha had sent a message to him that said, "Lord, your dear friend is very sick" (v. 3). In the days that followed, their helpless hearts broke as they watched their brother die.

In his account, the apostle John emphasizes the love Jesus had for this family (vv. 5, 36). Jesus had a special bond with Mary, Martha, and Lazarus. They were close friends who had shared life together. Their intimate relationship only added to the sisters' pain and confusion when Jesus did not immediately come to Lazarus's sickbed. Jesus had often seen fit to heal perfect strangers. He'd performed miracles before the masses many times. So why not this miracle? Why not for his dear friend?

Was it asking too much? Did he love them too little?

## APPROACHING JESUS WITH OUR PAIN

Are you, like Mary and Martha, wondering why Jesus hasn't kept you from this season of sorrow? Has the pain and confusion of your grief overwhelmed you with faith-related questions and doubts? Knowing that Jesus can keep sad things from happening but sometimes chooses not to is a difficult thought for any believer to process—let alone a person who is walking through depression.

This is why Mary and Martha's groans of grief have much to teach us. They show us how to cry out to Christ in our heartbreak.

Jesus and his disciples approached Lazarus's village a few days after receiving the sisters' message. Although Jesus already knew what would happen to his friend and had a plan to raise him back to life (John 11:4), the two women did not know his plan in the slightest. They just knew that their brother had died and Jesus hadn't been there to intervene.

Yet even though they knew Jesus could have healed their brother—and even though he did not—they went to Jesus with their grief instead of turning away from him in anger. Rather than giving him the silent treatment or the cold shoulder, they ran to their beloved friend and expressed their pain. Separately, each one told him, "Lord, if only you had been here, my brother would not have died" (John 11:21, 32).

## DIFFICULT THOUGHTS

Thoughts such as Mary and Martha's are hard for us to process —let alone to admit and speak aloud. Can you relate to their cry of mourning? Do any of the following statements give voice to your painful thoughts?

- If only Jesus had *helped* __________, this wouldn't have happened.
- If only Jesus had *healed* __________, this wouldn't have happened.
- If only Jesus had *delivered* __________, this wouldn't have happened.
- If only Jesus had *changed* __________, this wouldn't have happened.
- If only Jesus had *protected* __________, this wouldn't have happened.
- If only Jesus had *loved* __________, this wouldn't have happened.
- If only Jesus had (fill in what you hoped he'd do), this wouldn't have happened.

The day I went to the ER, I was thinking, "If only God had helped me, I wouldn't have been hospitalized like this again." But unlike Mary and Martha, I didn't dare to take these thoughts to Jesus. They seemed *too* honest. So I just suppressed and ignored them, having plenty of other thoughts to deal with at the time.

## WHAT ARE WE ALLOWED TO SAY?

Maybe this describes where you are with your sadness right now. Perhaps you're not only heartbroken by humanly unfixable problems but also experiencing a steady barrage of difficult thoughts. Maybe you're questioning God's goodness, doubting his wisdom, or fearing his sovereignty. If so, it's important to recognize that these difficult thoughts are a normal byproduct of suffering. It's true that faith is tested when we watch God's good gifts break before our eyes. It's hard to grieve with hope when you feel hurt by God (Prov. 13:12). And it's normal to doubt that our Lord is wise and good when he seems to be withholding the help we need.

But we need to remember that by God's grace, he invites us to bring our hurt and heartbreak to him. We are free to pour out the pain in our hearts (Ps. 62:8)—there are no thoughts too honest to share with a God who already knows them (Ps. 139:4). That's why it's important to see these sisters speak so plainly in their grief. They shoved neither their Savior nor their sorrow away.

## BRING HEARTBREAK TO GOD

In the previous chapter, we saw that God's mercy may be to show us how to live in the midst of weariness. Here he teaches us how to pray in the midst of sadness. Though it's tempting for us to ignore our grief or turn away from God in anger, biblical lament enables us to "receive mercy and find grace to help us in our time of need" (Heb. 4:16 NIV). Take a closer look at Martha's groan in its entirety:

> Martha said to Jesus, "Lord, if only you had been here, my brother would not have died. But even now I know that God will give you whatever you ask." (John 11:21–22)

Do you notice how different her words are from Moses's and Elijah's? Martha expresses her pain to Jesus *and* puts her trust in his character and plan. Although we do hear a complaint, we don't hear rage or resignation in her pain. When Martha laments, she expresses her sorrow while "at the same time revealing faith in the power of Jesus to heal."[3] Martha's desperate prayer is one of sadness and faith, of weeping and worship. She goes to Jesus with her grief, talks to him about her hurt, asks for help, then trusts him with the outcome. Though she doesn't know what will come next, she's confident Christ can bring forth good from their grief.

He's with them. He loves them. She has hope that he'll make everything right.

## DOUBTING THE PLAN

Do you struggle to believe that Christ can bring forth good from your grief today? Sometimes in our sadness, it's not that we doubt God *has* a plan for our lives but that we doubt his plan is the best one. Jesus works in unpredictable ways. What if he leads us to more hurt and heartbreak? Our Lord's sovereignty is a comfort only to the degree we believe he's also good and wise.[4] Maybe we're not sure about him anymore—not when grief is blurring our eyes.

Sister, if you're fighting to believe God is good and wise today—that he loves you and has a plan for the sad season you're in—you are not the only one. Real believers wrestle with doubts about God's character more often than we recognize or care to admit.

But when we are walking through depression in motherhood, we may struggle to engage such disorienting doubts at all. It may seem safer, easier, for us to suppress our pain or ignore our confusion altogether. And the more hesitant we are to turn to Jesus in our grief, the more quickly sadness will shut us down. Cameron Cole describes this problem well: "If you fail to face reality, you will deaden your soul. If you shut yourself off from the pain, you will lock out joy. If you refuse to enter the reality of your suffering, you will not be able to enter into the blessings of life. Your heart will become hardened and closed and unhealed. Distance will develop in your relationships, both human and divine."[5]

## LEANING INTO LAMENT

Somewhere along the line, I got it into my head that believers should never feel sad when processing difficult thoughts. As a result, my obedience gradually began to be motivated by a desire for an unrealistic outcome: grief-free living. After each descent into darkness, I'd redouble my efforts to not feel grieved in the wake of heartbreak. When this didn't work, I wondered why God wasn't helping me to be constantly happy—it seemed like a good and worthy goal for me to strive for.

Perhaps that's one reason that I felt utterly defeated by my hospitalization. Maybe that's why I felt humanly unfixable. I had set my hope on the prevention of sadness rather than the redemption of sadness—and that isn't the hope that Jesus Christ offers to us. He never promises us grief-free living. He never commands us to avoid feeling sad. Rather, he said our troubles would be many but our sorrow would turn to joy in time (John 16:20, 22). He said we would weep and lament in this life, but he encouraged us to take heart in him as we do (John 16:33).

We have hope in sorrow because Christ will redeem all our pain (Rev. 21:4).

Ultimately, my quest for emotional stability became an exercise in suppression and avoidance. And while much more could be said about sadness in depression, my main goal is to help you to see that you can lament to Jesus, however unnerving it might seem. And unlike Mary and Martha, you don't have to wait for Jesus to meet you in your mourning. You may be waiting on his plan to unfold, but you're not waiting on his presence to draw near. He's with you. He loves you. There's hope he'll make everything right.

So pour out your heart before him, sister. Christ offers himself as your refuge.

## AFTER DARKNESS, LIGHT

When we feel sad, God invites us to tell him of our hurt and heartbreak. By his merciful grace, you can take that step today. I've included guidance on practicing lament in the appendix so you can grow your fluency in these grief-filled prayers of pain. As you engage your Savior with your sorrow, let him remind you of his plan to make things right. *After darkness, I will bring you light; after death, I will bring you life.*[6]

> Jesus told her, "Your brother will rise again." (John 11:23)

What Martha and Mary didn't perceive about Jesus's plan was the God-glorifying outcome he had in mind for Lazarus—a resurrection (vv. 43–44). Though this plan may not have felt loving as it unfolded, we have the benefit of hindsight. Yes, before witnessing a joyous outcome the family experienced tremendous sorrow—a painful reality Christ neither diminished nor ignored (vv. 33–35). But every one of those heartbreaking, humanly unfixable moments fit into his good, gracious plan of redemption. He didn't leave his friends in the darkness of death. He brought them light and life, just as he promised.

"Jesus bought the right to make everything right."[7] We have hope even when everything's wrong.

## NEXT STEP

Tell Jesus about your pain, confusion, and sorrow through a prayer of lament.

*Trust in him at all times, you people; pour out your hearts to him, for God is our refuge. (Ps. 62:8* NIV*)*

## REMEMBER

When I feel sad about the heartbreaking troubles I face and it seems as though Jesus isn't around to help, I will not ignore or suppress my raw emotions but choose to pour out the hurt in my heart to him instead.

## REFLECTIONS FOR PERSONAL APPLICATION

1. Describe how you're feeling today. Did any words or phrases in this chapter resonate with your experience?
2. Note one insight you gleaned in this chapter about your experience of sadness.
3. Note one step you can take today to apply what you've learned in this chapter to your own situation.
4. What have you learned today about the mercy of God toward those who feel sad?

*4*

# ANGER

## *When Life Feels Unfair*

Does it feel like you *shouldn't* be walking through this darkness? That's how I felt after my first full day in the psychiatric hospital. Though I had admitted myself voluntarily, I didn't think I should have been there. I felt like God should've helped me to avoid this whole situation—like I should have known better than to sink into such despair. And now I was hospitalized—again? It didn't seem right. How was this love? How was this mercy?

If you feel like the darkness you're enduring is unfair—if you think God has "forgotten to be gracious" to you (Ps. 77:9)—Michelle knows what you're going through. The same night she blew out the candles on her cake, a fire blew through the kitchen in her house. Firefighters tried but were unable to save the home her late husband had built before he died.

Michelle felt like she had nothing left to live for. After decades of striving to be a faithful Christian wife and mother, she had become a displaced widow with a wayward son. She often wondered what she did wrong because none of it seemed fair to her. Sometimes she'd sob to God in anger over what was lost and what would never be: "Why have you been so cruel to me, God?! I thought you loved me!"

## AM I ANGRY?

If you had asked me if I was angry in the days leading up to my total meltdown, I would have denied it. But when, reading in my hospital bed, I encountered Ed Welch's observation that "sadness + anger = depression,"[1] I wondered if there was more to my despair than simply sorrow. It was a question that I hadn't asked before.

That anger can be a contributor *to* despondency rather than its byproduct may be a new observation to you. It was to me. At first, I wasn't sure what that could look like in the context of my story. Maybe you're wondering the same. If there is a hidden undercurrent of anger churning beneath our sadness, how can we discover it?

To start, it's helpful to realize what anger is: a feeling of displeasure in response to a real or perceived injustice. Perhaps the easiest way for us to spot it is to consider our words. What do we say when our circumstances run contrary to our expectations? What do we sound like when it seems as though God is withholding his help or when it feels like God has "slammed the door on his compassion" (Ps. 77:9)? Our words in these moments reflect our hearts (Luke 6:45). They act as windows to the soul.

Do you ever find yourself red-faced and sobbing, "Lord, what have I done? Why are you against me?!" Or, like Moses, exclaiming, "Why are you treating me, your servant, so harshly? Have mercy on me! What did I do to deserve [this]?" (Num. 11:11). Do you think that God should be working in your life much differently than he seems to be? Do you feel like God is getting your story wrong?

## WHEN LIFE FALLS APART

The book of Job recounts a mother's worst nightmare. In four separate but concurrent incidents, Job and his wife lose their livestock, servants, and all ten of their grown children to invaders and natural disasters (Job 1:13–19). To say they were *only* saddened by these losses is a significant understatement. One minute, Job and his wife had it all—the next, all their precious children and personal assets were gone. And, if that wasn't enough, Job soon became afflicted with severe boils "from the soles of his feet to the crown of his head" (Job 2:7 NIV).

What helplessness his grieving wife must have felt. Their life had fallen apart. All she could do was watch.

Perhaps you know what it's like to have your world turned upside down. Under the circumstances, it's not hard for us to understand why Job's wife encouraged her husband to renounce his faith and reproach his Creator. "Are you still trying to maintain your integrity?" she asks him. "Curse God and die" (Job 2:9).

Do you hear it? This mother's words make it clear. She's not only mourning her family's immense suffering and loss—she's incredibly angry about it too. The whole situation appears so cruel and unfair. Why hasn't God shielded them from these sorrows? What's the point of faithfulness, she exclaims, if the God they worship will treat them this way?

If there's ever a time for faith to be tested, it's when God allows us to lose what we love.

## THE ROAR OF RAGE AND THE CRY OF FAITH

Let's not be quick to judge Job's wife. Was this grieving wife and mother supposed to be calm, cool, and collected in the wake of such tragedy? Of course not! Would she have been wrong to *hate* what had happened to her family? No, not at all. Because God made us to be moral creatures with an innate sense of justice, anger is absolutely right to identify "some things [as] terribly wrong."[2] God did not originally create us to contend with such evils. He hates mankind's curse much more than we do.

In this way, our anger sometimes mimics God's own.

Thankfully, the Lord has given us a pathway to authentically engage him in our hurt and heartbreak. *Lament.* As we've seen, "when the Bible teaches [us] how to voice distress to God, it teaches a cry of faith, not a roar of rage."[3] The words of Job's wife were the latter—a guttural groan in a moment of weakness. In the midnight hour, she became "like a person who does not trust God . . . like someone who does not even know who God is."[4] In contrast, Job answered her with a cry of faith: "Should we accept only good things from the hand of God and never anything bad?" (Job 2:10).

Notice that Job's response doesn't gloss over the painful reality of his family's tragedy. What was happening to them was not "good" but "bad." It's helpful to hear this blameless, God-fearing man speak so plainly (Job 1:1). We don't need to call bad things "good" or bitter things "sweet" (Isa. 5:20). When our cries of faith are heartfelt and honest, it means we're worshipping in truth (John 4:24).

Having faith in the midst of heartbreak doesn't mean faking your way through the pain.

But notice something else: Job tells it like it is *without* saying God is wrong. Not only does he credit the Lord with "controlling both the delightful and the bitter things"[5] that happened in their lives, but he challenges his wife's outburst with a call to acceptance (Eccl. 7:14). He reminds her that God is God—his name is worthy to be blessed, even if they feel cursed (Job 1:21).

## RIGHT OR WRONG

The exchange between Job and his wife articulates questions that God's people have always struggled to answer: Is it right for a good and loving God to permit suffering? Is it wrong for him to take away what we love? Is he right to prosper the wicked and impoverish the faithful? Is it right to rage against God when he lets our lives fall apart (Jonah 4:9)? Are we wrong to judge the quality of God's love by the quantity of our sorrows (Eph. 3:18)?

Though we may know the "right" Christian responses to these questions, our hearts can struggle to connect the dots between the reality of our pains and the mystery of God's purposes. How can God be good when he lets us get hurt so badly? It's not uncommon for disillusionment to swell in the wake of devastation, as we see in Job's story.

The trouble is that anger fuels our disillusionment by answering faith-related questions on its own. Brad Hambrick explains, "Anger wastes no time in connecting dots. If there are two dots on the page—dot 1, I was hurt, and dot 2, God was involved—then anger hastily scribbles a bold line between them: God hurt me. God is not safe. Everything I was told about God was a lie."[6]

## RESTLESS FOR ANSWERS

It's normal to have questions about the tragic or painful parts of our stories. We want to know "Why me?" or "Why them?" or "Why this?" or "Why now?" or "Why not?" We may think the more answers we get, the more peace we'll find. But when our questions are many and God's answers are few, frustration may follow. The explanations we want are the ones we don't have (Dan. 4:35). Because we cannot know God's mind (Rom. 11:34). Because he has the right to keep secrets (Deut. 29:29). Because he is God and we are not.

Try as it might to draw right conclusions, anger cannot give us the comfort we're searching for (James 1:20).

As we continue through Job's story, we watch him become increasingly restless for answers about (and comfort in) his unbearable suffering (Job 3:23–26). We see him struggle, just like we do, to connect the dots between his suffering and his service to God. "Isn't calamity for the wicked and misfortune for those who do evil?" (Job 31:3). The longer he suffers, the more Job calls into question how the sovereign Lord has handled his situation. In the midst of his anguish, he groans, "My bitter soul must complain" (Job 7:11).

> I cry to you, O God, but you don't answer.
> I stand before you, but you don't even look.
> *You have become cruel toward me.*
> You use your power to persecute me.
> You throw me into the whirlwind
> and destroy me in the storm. (Job 30:20–22)

Maybe you can relate to how Job feels in this moment. Does it feel like God has become disinterested in you? *Cruel* to you? Like Job, do you sometimes wonder why God seems to treat you more like an enemy than a servant (Job 13:24)? Job couldn't stand it anymore—he had to know why God was against him. "Let the Almighty answer me," he roared (Job 31:35). In effect, one commentator writes, "he has challenged [the Creator of the Universe] to make his case in court."[7]

## ANGRY AT GOD

As I reflected upon the cries of my heart in the weeks leading up to my hospitalization, I began to see that I wasn't *just* sad about the direction my story had taken. I wasn't *only* grieved over my hurt and heartbreak or the many challenges my family faced. I hadn't faced the fact that I was mad as well—and not just at people for hurting me. Not just at myself for being a "failure" of a Christian wife and mother. I was angry at God for the story I was in.

I felt like he had become cruel to me. I couldn't understand why the Lord I loved would keep me trapped "in a prison of suffering, loneliness, pain, and misery."[8] I wanted so desperately to escape it, to be a strong and faithful believer. To be an overcomer whose life was falling into place instead of a struggler whose life was falling apart. But God seemed to be holding me back—seemed to be withholding his help.

My anger's hasty conclusion? God was against me. My faith was a lie.

Maybe you're wrestling with similar thoughts today. Do you harbor resentment at God for the sorrow you have or the story he's given you? Perhaps you've tried to be faithful in the face of your difficulties, but you're angry that God hasn't helped you to triumph over your troubles. We know he can, so why doesn't he? If he says he is for us, then why does it feels like he's against us (Rom. 8:31)? If he wants us to seek his face, why does he keep hiding it (Pss. 27:8; 88:14)? If he truly is our shield, why hasn't he shielded us from tragedy or trauma (Ps. 84:11)?

If he is a very present help, why won't he help us to break free from this prison of darkness (Ps. 46:1)?

## GOD CHALLENGES JOB

After Job calls the Almighty to account, God breaks his silence (Job 38:1–3). But he doesn't come to explain himself or give reasons for Job's suffering. Instead, he challenges his servant by turning the tables. God asks Job question after question about how the heavens are managed, how the world was made, and how all creation is cared for. This isn't just a *thorough* interrogation—it is a *terrifying* one.

"Do you still want to argue with the Almighty?" God asks his suffering servant. "You are God's critic, but do you have the answers?" (Job 40:2).

Commentator Christopher Ash explains that God "[challenges] Job's words. . . . Although at the very end God will affirm that Job has spoken rightly of him (42:7), Job has also said some very wrong things about God."[9] Hasty scribbles had been drawn in anger. Job's conclusions about God's disposition were not right. Maybe he thought he knew how life was supposed to work for God-fearers, but he discovered that he was mistaken. Before, he had only heard about God. Now, he had seen the Lord with his own eyes (42:5).

Not only did God's challenge give Job clarity, it paved the way to his comfort.

## THE MERCY OF REPENTANCE

As we consider how Job's story intersects with anger in depression, we glean several helpful insights. Yes, the man was grief-stricken—as you may be. Yes, he was experiencing excruciating suffering—as you may be. But Job also tried to connect the dots between his hurt and his God with an incomplete view of reality—as *we all* are tempted to do. If he was to be comforted in his grief and affliction, Job would have to think much differently about it. So God challenged Job into a change of mind. It was what he most needed at the time.

Finding fault with God is not the way to make sense of our sorrows.

Humbled by God's cosmic questions, Job expresses his change of mind with a cry of faith: "I take back everything I said, and I sit in dust and ashes to show my repentance" (Job 42:6). For Job, repentance was the very best step he could take at the apex of his angst. It was a step of humble acceptance underwritten by the mercy of his Maker. Despite all his wrong words, Job remained right with God by repenting of them. The Lord's challenge was an act of mercy. It brought Job the comfort he'd been searching for (Job 42:10–11).

## CHANGING OUR MINDS

If today you recognize an undercurrent of anger churning beneath your sadness, Job's story may illuminate your next step. To be challenged by God to change your mind through repentance *is* an act of mercy. He's inviting you to think differently—not just about his sovereign handling of your situation but also about how life in a fallen world really works for his children (Rom. 8:17; Eph. 1:5).

As we reflect on this, I want to draw your attention to the fact that Job's suffering was the result of his *right* relationship with God (Job 1:8). His life didn't fall apart because he had done something wrong. No! Devastating loss and disease fell upon him specifically *because* he was a believer. Although Job never knew it, Satan had attacked him because of his faith, claiming that the only reason Job blessed the Lord was that he led a blessed life (Job 1:9–10). "But reach out and take away everything he has," Satan suggests to God, "and he will surely curse you to your face" (Job 1:11).

Although God did not agree to reach out *his* hand against Job, he did permit his servant to be temporarily tested and tempted by *Satan's* evil hand (Job 1:12; 2:6). God demonstrated his sovereignty in the situation by setting limits to Satan's attack. Though Satan was not free to do his worst, he did tear Job's whole world apart for a while.

The exchange between God and Satan in heaven challenges us to change our minds about how we interpret suffering in our lives as Christians. The way we go about connecting the dots between our hurt and our Lord is especially critical in depression. We feel heartbroken. We're downcast and desperate for consolation. Yet sometimes the reason our hearts struggle to be comforted is that we've accepted anger's bold and hasty scribbles as irrefutable truth: "God has become cruel to me. I'm no longer safe in his hands."

Job's story shows us a much different reality.

Your suffering + God's silence ≠ God's hand is against you.

## WHAT YOU *CAN* KNOW

As you fight to change your mind about how God has sovereignly handled your situation, it will help to remember what you *can* know based on actual gospel truth, not anger's interpretation of reality. Before taking your next step, consider this observation from pastor and author Frederick S. Leahy: "In the case of Job God set a limit to Satan's activity. In the experience of Christ, there were no limits to Satan's onslaught. He was free to do his worst, and he did."[10]

The God who gave Job over to Satan's hand is the same God who gave *himself* over to Satan's limitless onslaught. He did this for the sake of his holy name and for the love of his covenant people (1 Sam. 12:22; Isa. 48:11). Your Lord humbly accepted Satan's worst so you would come to inherit God's very best (1 Peter 1:3–9). No, maybe you can't connect all the dots between your hurt and your Father in heaven, but you can rightly conclude that a God who suffers *for* you is not *against* you (Rom. 8:31–34).

As we consider the overall trajectory of the Christian life, let's remember that we are living in the middle of God's redemptive story. Just as Job's is a ruin-before-restoration story, and Christ's is a death-before-resurrection story, yours is a suffering-before-glory story, a hurt-before-healing story, a darkness-before-light story (Rom. 8:17). No matter how bad or bitter things seem today, you will not be left where you are now.

God will not keep you in this prison forever—that's not his plan.

## NEXT STEP

Lament your hurts and repent of wrong conclusions your anger has drawn about God.

*As you know, we count as blessed those who have persevered. You have heard of Job's perseverance and have seen what the Lord finally brought about. The Lord is full of compassion and mercy. (James 5:11* NIV*)*

## REMEMBER

When I feel angry about my sad story and it seems like God has become cruel toward me, I will remember that God hates evil and injustice more than I do, that my sorrows are not proof that God's hand is against me, and that true believers are called to share in Christ's earthly sufferings before they can share in his eternal glory.

## REFLECTIONS FOR PERSONAL APPLICATION

1. Describe how you're feeling today. Did any words or phrases in this chapter resonate with your experience?
2. Note one insight you gleaned in this chapter about your experience of anger.
3. Note one step you can take today to apply what you've learned in this chapter to your own situation.
4. What have you learned today about the mercy of God toward those who feel angry?

# 5

# ANXIETY

## *Searching for Certainty*

Sometimes our thoughts become consumed by what-if questions. When harassing hypotheticals swarm a person's mind, they create a fog she cannot see (or think) beyond. That's what I experienced after the psychiatrist left my hospital room. His diagnosis? Bipolar disorder II. His prescription? Pills and bloodwork. In the solitude that followed his visit, I grew increasingly worried over what this label would mean for my future. For every one uncertainty, there seemed to be a dozen what-ifs for me to answer. But the problem was, I couldn't. Every mental rabbit trail I wandered down was a path to nowhere.

Imani also experienced how crippling it can be to wrestle with what-if questions. After being diagnosed with major depressive disorder at the age of forty-one, she was afraid the vibrant life she used to have was over forever. She didn't know why she'd felt so sad for so long. She didn't know when she'd start to feel better again, if at all. All she knew was that, with four young children to raise, her current limitations did not match her life's demands. She felt like a burden to the ones she loved the most.

For Imani, the what-ifs were unrelenting—particularly at night when she was trying to fall asleep. As soon as she closed her eyes, the floodgate would open and the cares of the day would overwhelm her mind. Hours passed as she shuffled through endless internal dialogues. For a while she stopped going to bed altogether, choosing to stay up and watch TV on the couch instead. Eventually she'd nod off from sheer exhaustion. Skipping the pillow seemed like her best (and only) option.[1]

## WRACKED BY WHAT-IFS

What-if questions tend to decrease peace and increase panic. A tendency toward overanalysis can be paralyzing. A desire for answers—to know the who, what, where, when, why, and how in *all* our uncertainties—can lead to both restlessness and joylessness. Anxious thinking feels downright oppressive, "as if we are in a dark prison, enslaved in bars of fear."[2] As if peace is for everyone but us.

Does it sometimes feel like you're being held captive by worries and what-ifs? A fearful anticipation of the future inhibits our ability to enjoy God's peace in the present. Maybe we're afraid that past sorrows will repeat in the future. Perhaps we're scared that present sorrows will endure. Either way, the uncertainties of life can leave us feeling out of control, out of resources, and even out of breath. It's no wonder anxiety and depression often go hand-in-hand: "My soul is bereft of peace; I have forgotten what happiness is" (Lam. 3:17 ESV).

More than that, sometimes even our bodies feel like they're being held captive by fear. Although our instinct to fight, flee, or freeze in the presence of danger is God-given, these natural protection mechanisms become unnecessarily triggered at times when the only danger is imaginary, or remembered, or a product of sensory overload. Because we're embodied souls, it's common for psychological (inner) and physiological (outer) distress to intertwine—anxious thoughts feed off panicking bodies and vice versa. In addition, physical problems such as heart conditions, the amount of caffeine we consume, and side effects from medications can also set us on edge.[3]

For many mothers, anxiety is a whole-person experience.

Although what-ifs may not be the only things that are contributing to your anxious feelings today, they give us something meaningful to work with. They reveal what your heart truly treasures (Matt. 6:21). They expose what your heart truly trusts (Jer. 17:5–8). When they shine a light on your fears, you can see them for what they are and learn to respond accordingly.

## GIDEON'S ANXIOUS EXPERIENCE

In Scripture the Lord often interacts mercifully with fear-stricken people, of whom Gideon is one. In Judges 6, we find him processing his family's grain in secrecy (v. 11).

Gideon's fear had been conditioned by danger and loss. For seven long years, the nation of Midian "would come like locusts in number" to lay waste to the Israelites' land (v. 5 ESV). They stole harvests and terrorized the people. These foreign oppressors created an atmosphere of dread: "Israel was brought very low because of Midian" (v. 6 ESV). It's in the context of judgment and desperation that we find Gideon beating wheat in a sheltered winepress. A typical exposed threshing floor was simply an unsafe place to be.

Can you imagine the what-ifs that plagued this man's thoughts? *What if I'm discovered? What if our grain is stolen? What if our food runs out? What if my family is harmed? What if we're never delivered from our enemies?*

In the midst of Gideon's anxious toil, a messenger of the Lord suddenly appeared to him and said, "Mighty hero, the LORD is with you!" (v. 12). Gideon replied with a cynical groan. "If the LORD is with us, why has all this happened to us? And where are all the miracles our ancestors told us about? Didn't they say, 'The Lord brought us up out of Egypt'? But now the Lord has abandoned us and handed us over to the Midianites" (v. 13).

In the sunken perspective of Gideon's rock-hewn winepress, the future looked bleak. Gideon expressed both fear and resentment because, to him, nostalgic stories of God's past faithfulness were irrelevant to the crisis at hand.[4] If the hardships of the last seven years were any indication, it seemed that Israel could no longer depend on the Lord for help. It seemed like God had given up on his people—this time, for good.

## PAIN FUELS OUR FEAR

Could it be that what-ifs are tempting you to think like Gideon today? When you view your sorrows as proof of God's abandonment—if you believe you face tomorrow without his loving presence—then doom and gloom are a reasonable response. Like Gideon, you may feel a twinge of cynicism when a word of hope is spoken: *Are you kidding? If God is with me, then why has this happened? Where's his deliverance? He's abandoned me!*

Often today's fears are fueled by yesterday's pains. We've watched bad dreams turn into real-life nightmares, and it seemed like God was nowhere to be found. We cried out for a miracle. We received no reply. We don't know what to make of our suffering or God's perceived silence. If you've ever felt like the Lord left you to fight those battles alone—even after you trusted him for help—you're far from the only one (Pss. 10:1; 22:1–2; 88:13–14).

It can be hard to hope for the best when you've lived through a season of worsts (Lam. 3:18). And if we believe our past sorrows are any indication, we might think we can no longer depend on the Lord for help. Our hearts may harden against hope in order to avoid the pain of disappointment. Because *what if* we lose (or never get) what's important to us? What if God doesn't have our best interests at heart? What if he's good to other people—but not to us?

## WALKING INTO THE UNKNOWN

On top of our concerns and uncertainties, we also have our God-given responsibilities to consider. Inevitably, fulfilling those responsibilities requires that we walk by faith and not sight (2 Cor. 5:7) and that we step into the good works God has prepared for us to do while entrusting life's mysteries and surprises to him (Eph. 2:10). And therein lies the challenge. We don't want to walk into mysteries or surprises. We've been hurt before and we're afraid of experiencing that pain again. So when the Lord calls us to move forward to the next chapter in our story, we balk.

Turning the page can be scary when we don't know what's on it.

## MISSION IMPOSSIBLE?

The real tension created between concerns and responsibilities[5] is something we see reflected in Gideon's story as well.

It's interesting that the messenger who appeared to Gideon neither rebuked nor addressed his cynicism. Instead, he gave the anxious man a frightening job to do. For the next chapter in his story, God instructed Gideon to go and deliver Israel from the oppression of Midian. But this fresh assignment from heaven did nothing to ease Gideon's concerns. It only added to them! Instead of walking in the good work God had prepared for him, Gideon balked (Judges 6:14–15).

To be fair, Gideon was being called to a dangerous endeavor. It seemed like an impossible task, and the logistics made no earthly sense whatsoever. Maybe that describes where you are at in your story. The future you're being called into looks scary and nonsensical—*impossible,* even. And though part of you really wants to believe that God is good and that he knows what's best for your life, you're still afraid. If suffering comes, how will you bear it? How could you cope with more heartbreak and pain? The thought of getting through an uncertain tomorrow is overwhelming when we're barely making it through the problems of today.

## WILL GOD GET IT RIGHT?

As we saw in the previous chapter, sometimes we feel angry because it seems like God has given us the wrong story. When this anger goes unrecognized, unacknowledged, or unconfessed, disillusionment and bitterness result. But if "bitterness is believing God got it wrong," we might also say that "worry is not believing God will get it right."[6]

This was the tension in which Gideon was caught. He was cynical because of the past and worried because of the future, frustrated by God's perceived abandonment and frightened by the terrifying task ahead.

Do you feel this inner tension yourself? Are you anxious about moving forward in your story because you fear God won't get the next chapter right? Are you afraid of being left alone or let down? Afraid of falling to pieces again? If this is your struggle, read on. We're about to see divine assurance interact with human apprehension in the most merciful way.

## SHOW ME A SIGN

Gideon wasn't sure he wanted to turn the page in his story—at least, not without some guarantees. Allow me to paraphrase his response in Judges 6:14–18:

God: Go with the strength you have—I am sending you!

Gideon: But Lord, how can I?

God: I will be with you.

Gideon: If you are truly going to help me, show me a sign.

The words of this "mighty hero" are revealing. He wanted to know how his story was going to play out. He didn't understand how he could do what God commanded. He needed to be certain that the Lord was going to help him face the future, especially when he felt like he'd been abandoned for the past seven years. Desiring proof that God would do just as he promised, Gideon anxiously demanded to see a sign. He needed to be sure of the Lord's favor and presence—to know that God Almighty could be trusted.

## LOOKING FOR PEACE

I don't know about you, but Gideon's nervousness resonates with me. Called to reenter the world with a fresh psychiatric diagnosis, I balked. The bipolar label indicated that my future was hopeless—at least, that's what it seemed like from my sunken perspective. Hypotheticals swarmed my mind so intensely I could barely breathe. And I groaned just as Gideon did, "Lord, how can I possibly face this? If you are truly going to help me, would you show me a sign?"

In the hours that followed, I felt increasingly like a scared and helpless child left to fend for herself. I couldn't know how this was going to play out in my life and ministry. I'd already felt like God had given up on me. Why should I expect him to help me now? And how could I trust him to do what he said when all these weeks it seemed like he wouldn't? I needed something certain to look at just then—reassurance that he would go with me into the future I feared.

Remarkably, the Lord agreed to give Gideon the sign he asked for (Judges 6:18). After receiving confirmation of God's presence and favor, Gideon took his next step (vv. 19–24). Convinced that God would be true to his word, he "built an altar to the Lord there and named it Yahweh-Shalom (which means 'the Lord is peace')" (v. 24).

Assured of God's committed presence, Gideon took courage, and then he turned the page (v. 23).

Now, am I saying you should ask God for a sign as a cure for your anxiety? Not at all. In bringing us to this story, my main goal is that we see the mercy God gives to those who are frightened by the future they face. Do you see how God encouraged Gideon in his uncertainty? He gave the anxious man a sure sign. He patiently listened to Gideon's doubts and then proved that he could be trusted. The Lord would do all he had promised. Gideon could go because God was with him.

## THE SIGN

Maybe today you need a sign that God will go with you into the future you fear. I needed a sign, and he knew it—he knows every believer needs a sign. There can be no peace for his people without one! But sister, if you want to be certain that God can be trusted as you walk through this season of darkness, remember the sign that's been given to you—it's a far better one than Gideon saw.

If you find yourself wanting to be absolutely sure that God will help you—if you need assurance that he hasn't given up on you in the least—perhaps your next step forward is to look at the sign he gave: his Son (1 John 4:9–10). "All right then, the Lord himself will give you the sign. Look! The virgin will conceive a child! She will give birth to a son and will call him Immanuel (which means 'God is with us')" (Isa. 7:14). When what-ifs come to mind, we can call to mind *this* sign and trust Immanuel is with us—despite all our fears (Matt. 28:20).

It's true that we're called to walk by faith through depression (2 Cor. 5:7). It's true that God often makes us travel down roads that may surprise or even terrify us. But it's equally true that our merciful Lord has given a sign to reassure us—a "bright morning star" we can see even from our sunken perspective (Rev. 22:16). Beholding this sign, this star, this Son, is a priority for us when hypotheticals swarm. And with the help of the Holy Spirit, we can learn to behold him more and more quickly (John 14:26–27).

"Because of God's tender mercy," we've been given evidence that he can be trusted to do just as he promised (Luke 1:78). We're not to base God's trustworthiness on our circumstances but on the Son he's provided for salvation. Jesus took on human form for our sake. He knows how it feels to be afraid (Luke 22:41–44, Phil. 2:8; Heb. 2:14; 4:15). But he's also delivered us from a truly frightening future, to be certain (Matt. 13:49–50). He's committed to be with you now, always, and forever (Josh. 1:9; Matt. 28:20). Not once has Jesus lied to his people—not once has he "promised and not carried it through" (Num. 23:19).

God is surely with you—take courage and go where he guides.

## NEXT STEP

Instead of rehearsing what-ifs, meditate on Christ's promise to be present with you, no matter where you go.

*But when I am afraid, I will put my trust in you.* (Ps. 56:3)

## REMEMBER

When I feel anxious about the future and what-ifs begin to swarm my mind, I will not lean on my own faulty understanding but on a faithful Savior who'll stay by my side, whatever comes next.

## REFLECTIONS FOR PERSONAL APPLICATION

1. Describe how you're feeling today. Did any words or phrases in this chapter resonate with your experience?
2. Note one insight you gleaned in this chapter about your experience of anxiety.
3. Note one step you can take today to apply what you've learned in this chapter to your own situation.
4. What have you learned today about the mercy of God toward those who feel anxious?

# 6

# SHAME

## *Desperate to Be Different*

There are days when we feel set apart in the worst kind of way. For every sorrow, there seems to be a label: depressed, widowed, disabled, bereaved, victimized, disordered, separated, imprisoned, barren, diseased, poor, divorced, post-abortive, and on and on. And for every one of these labels, there seems to be an unshakable stigma—a signal of social difference or disgrace.

I recall distinctly feeling like an "other" as I stood in the hospital cafeteria line, shuffling forward with my eyes glued to the ground. I didn't want to be viewed as one of "those" women in the eyes of the dinner shift workers. Yet there I was. A mother on the margins, exposed for all to see. I felt freshly tagged as less than desirable. Flagged as a difficult woman to love.

Lin knows how painful these feelings can be. She struggled to silence the voice of shame after her sexual assault in college—a voice that insisted she was a "good-for-nothing girl," just like her dad had said when she was a child. When Lin finally worked up the courage to share her secret with her future husband, she feared she was permanently spoiled in his eyes. Despite his earnest assurances, she felt contaminated and defined by her past. It was almost as if her father had been right all along.

Since she couldn't silence the voice of shame, Lin did everything she could to prove it wrong. Seven years into her marriage, she found herself striving to be the "perfect" wife and mom. Not one for sitting still, she always kept herself, her house, and her adopted twin girls photo-ready. But try as she might to project a photogenic life, her public smiles only masked private sorrows. She could never shake her sense of being weighed and found wanting. "Good enough" is never enough when you think you're good for nothing.

## KNOWN BY SHAME

The labels and stigmas in our stories often leave unsightly marks, and some don't seem to fade with time. The resulting shame can be hard to shake. It haunts us like a shadow and continually whispers in our ears that we're unacceptable, untouchable, and unlovable.[1] Set apart by failure and disgrace. Unworthy through and through.

Do you ever think that if you could just be a different person, you'd be more worthy of love and acceptance? Shame speaks descriptively, convincingly, and degradingly about our every fault and flaw. It knows our deep secrets. It thrives in dark shadows. It insists that nothing in the present day can erase the dirt of yesterday because good deeds can never clean deep stains (Isa. 64:6).

Shame is the bass line in depression's dirge. Try as we might, we can't muffle its low-pitched sound for long. Maybe that's because shame pulses with truth. It knows who we really are. It's seen what we've really done. It's recorded our monstrous moments and remembers our destructive words. And if that wasn't enough, it's witnessed every wickedness done to us. Should anyone find out what we're hiding, it says, we'll be ruined. Forsaken.

Do you fear that some of your secrets will be discovered? Do you think you're damaged goods? Has the shame of your unspeakable or unshakable stains left you feeling "set apart with the dead" (Ps. 88:5 NIV)?

## SHAME AND DESPERATION

Shame can propel us to withdraw from the world, or even from God. Out of hopeless desperation, we may find ourselves wishing to "disappear or die, which are extreme versions of hiding."[2] Think back to Elijah. Remember how on one of his hard days, he disappeared into the wilderness alone and told God, "Take my life, for I am no better than my ancestors" (1 Kings 19:4). We hear similar notes in Job's groans as well:

> If I am guilty—woe to me! Even if I am innocent, I cannot lift my head, for I am full of shame and drowned in my affliction. . . . I wish I had died before any eye saw me. If only I had never come into being. (Job 10:15, 18–19 NIV)

Those are cries to disappear or die. From God's own well-regarded servants, no less!

Where suffering and shame mix, despair can result. But must our stains always lead to hopeless desperation? Is there anywhere else for us to go but *away*?

## A SUFFERING WOMAN'S SHAME

The story of the bleeding woman in Mark 5 is an ideal case study for us to explore as we consider these questions. Here we see a woman who lived on the margins of society. According to Jewish purity laws, her chronic menstrual discharge made her ceremonially unclean (Lev. 15:19–30). Like a leper, she could neither touch nor be touched—all she came into contact with was instantly contaminated. Not only did her illness make her socially unacceptable, but it also made her legally untouchable and physically unlovable (Lev. 20:18). As a result, this woman was ostracized. Banned from community. Barred from the temple. Prevented from practicing her faith. And she lived like this for twelve long and lonely years. It was barely a life at all.[3]

Not only had legal separation from God and his people set her apart in the very worst way (Num. 5:1–3), but "she had suffered a great deal from many doctors, and over the years she had spent everything she had to pay them, but she had gotten no better. In fact, she had gotten worse" (Mark 5:26). Her condition was heartbreaking and humanly unfixable. After all those years of exhausting her dwindling strength and limited resources, she continued to be dirtied daily. Her embarrassing malady could not be cured. The temple priest could not declare her "clean."

No healing, no cleansing, no community. Can you imagine how weary and worried she must have been? How sad and angry she must have felt at times? After so much effort to be different for the better, she remained different for the worse.

Perhaps we can relate to this sufferer's plight. Did she loathe her illness and the mark it had left on her life? Did she hate the separation it had created in her personal relationships? We don't know. We just know that when *our* attempts at self-improvement fail—when our quest for healing or change appears fruitless—we can be tempted to hate ourselves for the condition we're in.

It's disheartening to be different for the worse when all you want is to be different for the better.

## HOPEFUL AND DESPERATE

When the woman in our passage heard about Jesus—that he "had healed many people that day, so all the sick people eagerly pushed forward to touch him" (Mark 3:10)—she had an immediate choice to make. Would she leave the confines of her quarantine and risk humiliation for restoration? Or would she stay hidden away for fear of embarrassment and rebuke?

As we see in this scene, she resolved to go straight to Jesus. The woman was desperate *and* hopeful. There was nothing left to lose but her nerve.

> She had heard about Jesus, so she came up behind him through the crowd and touched his robe. For she thought to herself, "If I can just touch his robe, I will be healed." (Mark 5:27–28)

What a scene! For this untouchable woman to "contaminate" the crowd was bad enough—but to make a move toward Jesus from behind and touch *him*? Now that's desperation! And yet, as one commentator suggests, "There is no hint of cynicism or resignation in her story. Fear did not prevent her from acting in hope."[4]

*Fear did not prevent her from acting in hope.*

We have seen examples of hopeless desperation in previous chapters. But here we find an example of desperation and hope in coexistence. When we're tempted to hide, there *is* somewhere else to go but away. Shame needn't propel us to despair. Another option exists.

## WHAT MAKES THE DIFFERENCE?

So what is this other option? What makes the difference between hopeless and hopeful desperation? Before we tease out this contrast, let's first consider the woman's statement: "If I can just (do this), then I will be (this)." Do those words sound familiar? Have you ever said something like that? Do you ever think that if you could just be someone "better" or something "more," you'd finally be welcomed and wanted? You wouldn't be one of "those" difficult to love women anymore, and the voice of shame would be silenced? Perhaps you've suffered a great deal from the notion that if you could just figure out

- how to be a better mom, you would be approved.
- how to be a better wife, you would be commendable.
- how to be a better Christian, you would be worthy.
- how to be a better friend, you would be valuable.
- how to be more intelligent, you would be distinguished.
- how to be more healthy, you would be useful.
- how to be more attractive, you would be desirable.
- how to be more successful, you would be validated.

The list above prompts us to consider how much we have suffered and spent just to be different. All of this effort and for what? The fact is we're still dirtied daily. Shame keeps on shadowing us, whispering about our every fault and flaw. Despite our striving to be different for the better, we feel only different for the worse.

Although the suffering woman's words may sound familiar, they are not like the groans above. The object of this woman's faith was Jesus, not herself. Though she might have heard little about Christ's character (and even less about his message), she believed that *he alone* was the key to her restoration. Biblical counselor Ed Welch writes, "Desperation is one of the main ingredients of faith. Faith means you need healing, you can't do it yourself, and you are confident that Jesus is the hands-on Healer."[5]

Our faith can deepen as we let desperation drive us to Jesus.

## DOUBTS

But that's the trouble sometimes. Perhaps you aren't confident that Jesus is your personal, hands-on Healer. "If he is," you might wonder, "why isn't he healing me? Why isn't he helping me to change?" Even though you've heard how Jesus cared for the ostracized and stigmatized (Mark 2:16–17)—even though you've heard of his affinity for "those" kinds of people—you may doubt he has such an affinity for you. "Why would he waste his time on someone like me?"

Sister, I want you to know that if shame and self-loathing are dominating your inner dialogue, then your Savior's voice is missing from the conversation. To hear what he really has to say to you today, you have an important choice to make. Will you leave your hiding places to approach him—will you come to him now with nothing but your stains? Or will fear prevent you from acting in hope—from the kind of desperation that can change you *forever*?

## JESUS MAKES THE DIFFERENCE

For this suffering woman in this moment, there was no better step she could take than to come to Jesus for healing. And as soon as her hand, in faith, made contact with his clothes, our Lord's divine power was engaged. Her bleeding immediately stopped; Jesus froze right where he stood (Mark 5:29).

> Jesus realized at once that healing power had gone out from him, so he turned around in the crowd and asked, "Who touched my robe?"
>
> His disciples said to him, "Look at this crowd pressing around you. How can you ask, 'Who touched me?'"
>
> But he kept on looking around to see who had done it. (Mark 5:30–32)

Notice that while Jesus desired intimacy, the woman desired secrecy. She blended in with the crowd. She came to him from behind. Maybe she thought she could get what she needed from Jesus and then quietly slip away unnoticed. But if this woman expected that she would be unpursued by Jesus in her condition, she was wrong. She might have been a no-status "other" to the people of her town, but Jesus didn't view her as one of "those" women. She wasn't so set apart by her sickness as to escape Christ's concern or attention—even if she thought she was or hoped she might be.

Rather, Jesus *noticed* her touch. He wanted to see her face-to-face. Although he had been on his way to help a high-status leader named Jairus, engaging the one who had reached out to him in faith became Christ's number-one priority. He wouldn't move forward from this spot without speaking to her first. So he kept on looking for her, until she "came and fell at his feet" (Mark 5:33 NIV).

This woman did not know Jesus's character like we do. She had no idea what he would say or do next. And yet, though her nerves were shaking, she testified to her embarrassing malady and miraculous healing. Yes, she had broken the law. Yes, she was chronically impure. But she had put all her hope in Jesus. He was not going to put her to shame (Rom. 5:5).

> And he said to her, "Daughter, your faith has made you well. Go in peace. Your suffering is over." (Mark 5:34)

## THE LORD IS OUR HIDING PLACE

Have you ever thought, "I don't know how God can still love me—*I* don't even love me!"? I have. When the disorder diagnosis seemed to set me apart as one of "those" women, I became haunted by shame and self-loathing. I felt unclean and unworthy. I thought Jesus was just as ashamed of me as I was of myself.

Shame came through the fall and is common to everyone, but depression can amplify its voice. If it feels like shame is dominating your inner dialogue today, the next step you can take is to let Jesus speak back on your behalf. Turn to the Scriptures. Discern *his* voice from the clamor in your mind (Heb. 12:24). Because Jesus doesn't speak mercilessly like other people do to one another, like Satan does, or like we do to ourselves. Rather, our Lord is a refuge for all of us who feel "other"—a shelter far from shame's accusing tongue (Ps. 31:20). Because he suffered a great deal to bear all our reproach—because he spent his blood to wash us "white as snow" (Isa. 1:18)—Jesus is our true and better hiding place (Pss. 22:6–7; 32:7). Our faith rests in his spotless perfection, not our own.

When it comes to engaging shame in depression, we're helped by the reminder that Christ (not us) is the object of our faith, that his righteousness (not ours) is the object of our confidence, that his healing (not our hiding) is the object of our hope. And as the bleeding woman's desperation shows, faith "derives its value not from the one who expresses it, but from the object in which it rests."[6]

This is good news for us as we walk through this season of sorrow. It means faith is objective, not resting on feelings, perceptions, or opinions, but on the unchanging truth of who Jesus is and the difference he's made in our status before God. Christ has called us by name, cleansed all our stains, and covered us with fine new clothes (Isa. 43:1; Zech. 3:4). By faith in him, we're warmly welcomed into his forever family. By his mercy, it is well with our souls—no matter what shame has to say (Rom. 8:33).

Although we don't have the authority to answer shame's merciless accusations, Jesus does. Rather than repel our Lord or compel him to treat us with contempt, our stains *propel* him to draw near to cleanse us. However dirty or damaged you feel today, Jesus is not ashamed to call you his sister (Heb. 2:11). He'll hold you close when no one else will (Ps. 27:10). His love has made you different for the better (Rom. 5:8–9).

Different forever (Rom. 8:30).

Sister, go forward in peace. Christ has set you apart in the best kind of way (1 Peter 2:9).

## NEXT STEP

Approach Jesus and let him speak with final authority to your shame through his Word.

*Do not be afraid; you will not be put to shame. Do not fear disgrace; you will not be humiliated. You will forget the shame of your youth and remember no more the reproach of your widowhood. (Isa. 54:4* NIV*)*

## REMEMBER

When I feel shame and am tempted to berate myself or hide away from the world, I will not let fear prevent me from acting in hope but will take refuge in the merciful cover of Christ's righteous robe.

## REFLECTIONS FOR PERSONAL APPLICATION

1. Describe how you're feeling today. Did any words or phrases in this chapter resonate with your experience?
2. Note one insight you gleaned in this chapter about your experience of shame.
3. Note one step you can take today to apply what you've learned in this chapter to your own situation.
4. What have you learned today about the mercy of God toward those who feel ashamed?

# 7

# LONELINESS

## *A Painful Paradox*

Depression feels indescribable. How many times have I struggled to explain to someone what this darkness is like? And how many tears have I cried because others rejected my answers as unreasonable, unbelievable, or unrelatable? By the time I sat waiting for the hospital's mandatory group counseling session to begin, I was tired of explaining. It seemed much easier to keep to myself.

Many women know what it's like to be misunderstood or mishandled in their sorrow—women like Brooke, whose first son, Timothy, was stillborn at thirty-eight weeks. Never had she felt as empty as the day she left the hospital without her baby. When people saw her about town weeks later and asked how the baby was doing, she fumbled to answer. Stillbirth seemed too big a topic for small talk. She tired of explaining what had happened and of suffering the unhelpful comments that sometimes followed.

When the condolences and meal trains ended after Timothy's funeral, friends and family seemed to increase their distance. Some dropped sympathy cards in the mail, while others said nothing at all. Everyone else was moving on with their life, but all Brooke wanted was to go back in time. To smell the hair and kiss the cheek of the boy who made her a mom.

In the valley of the shadow of death, Brooke became a shadow of her former self. No one could help her to "feel better." Her pain was too deep, her heart too broken.

## THE PARADOX OF LONELINESS

Do you sometimes feel like nobody "gets" you—like no one truly understands all that you're going through on this midnight journey? Because of the pain of being misunderstood or mishandled, we may shrug people off as a means of self-protection. Sometimes it seems easier to disengage than to face questions like "Is everything okay?" or "Did something happen?" or "What's the matter with you?"

Have you ever said, "I'm fine," because "I'm miserable" seems too off-putting for polite conversation?

Then again, sometimes *we* feel like the ones who are being shrugged off or pushed away. There are times when we groan, "My close friends detest me. Those I loved have turned against me" (Job 19:19); times when we've "looked for sympathy, but there was none" (Ps. 69:20 NIV); times when we think, "No one cares a bit what happens to me" (Ps. 142:4); times when we feel repulsive to others (Pss. 31:11; 88:8).

In these ways, loneliness in depression can be a paradox. On the one hand, we push people away. On the other, we wonder why they don't seem to care anymore. It is a miserable paradox to want nothing more than for people to leave us *and* to hold us at the very same time.

## FEELING EMPTY

Though loneliness can stem from physical separation from others, there's much more to it than being literally alone. Loneliness can also be a symptom of being disconnected from God and his people, relationally or emotionally. In the Scriptures, *lonely* can also be translated as *desolate*—as if we're not just alone, but our whole world feels empty.

If there's any mother in God's Word who knows what it's like to feel alone and empty, it's Naomi. After tumbling through a decade of tragedy in a foreign land, she went from being a married mother to a childless, destitute widow. Scripture tells us, "Naomi was left without her two sons and her husband" (Ruth 1:5 NIV).

The deaths of Naomi's husband and sons *left her without*. Think about the reality of that phrase for a moment. She was left without her spouse's companionship and love. Left without the financial support she needed. Left without a family unit to serve and belong to. Left without the mundane conversations that make up everyday life, and without heirs or obvious prospects for future flourishing. She was left without the ability to kiss and hug her only children. So when we read that Naomi had been left without, we need to remember just how much she had lost.

Her whole world, it seems. Her whole world.

## LEFT WITHOUT

Do you also feel like you've been left without someone or something important in this season of life? Maybe someone you once had—a husband, child, friend, sibling, or family member—is no longer in your life, or someone you've dreamed of hasn't turned up yet, or someone you have isn't willing (or able) to be the companion you want them to be. To be left without the person you've loved or longed for is to feel incomplete. Like an important—a necessary—piece of you is missing.

It's right for us to acknowledge this pain; the heartbreak it produces is worthy of our tears. God created us not to be left alone or left without but rather to love and be loved all our lives. To flourish in the context of meaningful relationships with him and his people.

And yet, the curse has corrupted God's design for our relational flourishing. Counselor Jayne Clark reminds us of what went wrong: "When Adam and Eve sinned, the perfect union they had enjoyed with God and with each other was destroyed. . . . Where once there had been openness, sin made for hiding. Where once there had been completeness, sin made for loss. Where once there had been acceptance, sin made for rejection. Where once there had been praise, sin made for blame. Hiding. Loss. Rejection. Blame. Ingredients of loneliness. Loneliness was born at the Fall."[1]

Being *left without* can manifest in other, less obvious ways as well. Sometimes it's not only that we feel like our world has been emptied—not only like we've been left without someone we've loved or longed for—but also that we have nothing of value to offer anyone. Like we have nothing positive to contribute to the world, let alone to the lives of the people we know.

Depression can leave us feeling bereft and bankrupt—left without purpose and worth.

## GOING ALONE

We see this dynamic at work in Naomi's story. She wasn't the only person to be left without. Her two daughters-in-law, Orpah and Ruth, had also become childless widows. And although "widowhood often meant inevitable alienation and destitution,"[2] Orpah and Ruth weren't entirely without prospects. From a social perspective, these younger women still had something left to offer. Each had her own mother's house to go back to and serve in (Ruth 1:8); Lord willing, they still had time to remarry and bear children of their own.

But these weren't options for elderly Naomi. So bleak did the future look from her grief-stricken perspective that when she decided to return to her hometown, she insisted on going alone in spite of Orpah and Ruth's desire to come. "Naomi replied, 'Why should you go on with me? Can I still give birth to other sons who could grow up to be your husbands?'" (Ruth 1:11).

Do you ever feel more like a liability to your loved ones than an asset? As if you're bringing them down or ruining their lives or spoiling their opportunities for future happiness? If so, you know something of what Naomi may have felt. Left without anything to offer Orpah and Ruth but a share in her misery, she told them to go home. After all, why should Naomi allow her alienation and destitution to become their problem? What difference would it make? Why waste their time on an old woman who had nothing left to offer them in return?

Perhaps we could summarize Naomi's words with one common phrase . . .

*Why bother?*

## WHY BOTHER?

To their credit, both Orpah and Ruth initially resisted Naomi's *why-bother* pushback (1:10). However, after she tearfully rebuked the young women and argued "the hopelessness of their staying with her,"[3] Orpah reluctantly obeyed and walked away.

Maybe this scene seems familiar. Perhaps we know what it's like to push people away with a shrug ("Why bother?") or even a rebuke ("Just leave me alone!"). Perhaps we've argued against their concern because

- we think they're wasting their time.
- we believe we're a hopeless case.
- we fear being viewed as weak and needy.
- we don't like to feel indebted to other people.
- we're afraid of being misunderstood or mishandled by others.
- we feel unworthy or undeserving of love.
- we feel left without anything of value to offer in return.

Naomi's story prompts us to consider if our *why bothers* reveal something important about our own despondent hearts. Although many mothers feel lonely at times, loneliness in depression often commingles with feelings of worthlessness and hopelessness, emptiness and resignation. It's not only that we feel alone and left without. It's not only that we feel misunderstood or mishandled. There seems to be no point in trying to connect with people anymore. Relationships feel more like a burden than a blessing to all involved.

And yet, try as we might to suppress or ignore it, we still find ourselves aching for love—especially in our most unlovable moments. Something deep within us longs to be embraced by someone who'll insist on bothering—who'll keep caring and coming around in spite of us. Yes, we can be prickly and hard to hold at times. No, we may not always make for pleasant company. But what would it mean for us today if someone cupped our cheeks in their hands, looked us straight in the eyes, and said, "I'm committed to you. Whatever comes next, we'll face it together"?

The world, it seems. It would mean the world.

## A FRIEND WHO STICKS CLOSE

To Naomi's surprise, she had a friend who "sticks closer than a brother" (Prov. 18:24). Ruth insisted on staying put in spite of her mother-in-law's *why bother* arguments (Ruth 1:14). Her heartfelt appeal to Naomi was as sacrificial as it was profound. "Don't urge me to leave you or to turn back from you. Where you go I will go, and where you stay I will stay" (v. 16 NIV). Whatever came next—be it danger or destitution—Ruth vowed that they would face it together.

Hopeless resignation can be dangerously isolating, which is why the days we least feel like having a friend around may be the days we most need one with us. Could that be why a lack of companionship in this season heaps misery upon misery? Maybe we don't really want to be left all alone (at least, not for very long)—we just don't want to become a burden or to be asked what's wrong with us all the time. It's hard to tell someone that their silent yet steady presence is the best kind of help they can give.

Precious is the friend who can sit by your side without so much as a word (Job 2:11–13).

## CHANGED BY GRIEF

At this point in Naomi's story, grief and hardship had taken their toll. As one commentator observes, this widow "who had left Bethlehem as Naomi, 'the pleasant one,' a robust woman in her prime, had returned as a haggard and destitute old woman."[4] Maybe that sounds a bit harsh, but when Naomi came back to her hometown, it seems she was nearly unrecognizable. Her reappearance after a decade-long absence was the buzz of the town. Upon her arrival, she was confronted with the uncomfortable question: "Is it really Naomi?" (Ruth 1:19).

Do you know what it's like for sorrow and hardship to take their toll on your countenance? And for people to notice? I do, and I hated being pressed for explanations. Who wants to describe all the reasons why she's not smiling and laughing like she used to?

Yes, walking through this season has changed us. We may never go back to the women we used to be. Not everyone understands that kind of personal grief, and it's hard to even know how to explain it. Sometimes we feel sick and tired of trying. We avoid familiar places or withdraw from those who know us best. We know that if we're seen, we'll be asked uncomfortable questions, and we won't know how best to answer them. Why bother with these interactions when we know how hard or hurtful they can be?

Although we don't always know how to put our misery into words, we know how to tell people to leave us alone. Perhaps we snap and spell it out for them explicitly or imply it through our passive disengagement, but no matter the manner with which it's communicated, the point we make is crystal clear: Why bother trying to help me? You can't fix this kind of problem!

And maybe that's what makes Naomi's response to the women's question so relatable for us today. Because it's almost as if she snapped and spelled it out. As if the years of grief and hardship finally came to a head and the ones within earshot got an earful:

> "Don't call me Naomi ['the pleasant one']," she responded. "Instead, call me Mara ['the bitter one'], for the Almighty has made life very bitter for me. I went away full, but the LORD has brought me home empty. Why call me Naomi when the LORD has caused me to suffer and the Almighty has sent such tragedy upon me?" (Ruth 1:20–21)

## BROKEN AND ALONE

Perhaps Naomi's words give voice to what some of our hearts are groaning today. Our whole world has gone from full and sweet to empty and bitter. All that once glimmered with light and life has now molded with darkness and death. After everything we've been through—after all we've been left without—we may groan along with Naomi that we have been "cruelly marred"[5] by the Almighty. Mercilessly broken by God.

In all the other narratives we've explored, the Lord came close to his desperate people. He engaged with the suffering of Moses, Elijah, Martha, Mary, Job, Gideon, and the bleeding woman by responding to their groans. Yet not once did God directly comfort or counsel Naomi. She didn't see him, or hear from him, or converse with him like the others did. All Naomi could perceive of God was that he'd mercilessly emptied her world (Ruth 1:13). It seemed she was destined for alienation and destitution.

## FORSAKEN

That God records Naomi's words in Scripture means he knows what desperate mothers sound like in their misery. He knows we sometimes feel as though he's squashing us like bugs. He knows how disoriented we become when we look to him for sympathy and seem to find none. He knows when we think he doesn't care about the darkness we're in. He knows when we feel abandoned in affliction.

But if God knows all this about us, why does he seem to remain silent (Ps. 35:22)? Why is he so far away when we groan for help (Ps. 22:1)? Why does he hide himself in times of trouble (Ps. 10:1)?

These questions reveal the deepest facet of the loneliness we may feel in depression. It's not just that we've been mishandled and misunderstood by other people. It's not just that we feel left without a devoted companion or anything of value to offer anyone. It's also that we feel left without God's loving presence in our lives. It's like we've been disowned and forsaken.

Our sense of forsakenness seems to be affirmed as we see others flourishing around us. God appears to be attentive to *their* prayers, to be blessing *their* lives, to be doing awe-inspiring ministry through *their* labors. But what about our prayers, lives, and labors? Like Naomi, we may believe that the Lord can be gracious, compassionate, and merciful to everyone else (Ruth 1:8–9). But when it comes to God's specific dealings with and disposition toward us as unique individuals, our miseries suggest that

(1) his sovereignty is without grace,
(2) his omnipotent power is without compassion, and
(3) his judicial will is without mercy.[6]

Sister, every step we've taken thus far together has led us to this critical crossroads.

Do God's midnight mercies seem to be for everyone but you?

## NEXT STEP

Refuse the suggestion that your sorrows are indicative of God's character.

*Though he brings grief, he will show compassion, so great is his unfailing love. For he does not willingly bring affliction or grief to anyone. (Lam. 3:33 NIV)*

## REMEMBER

When I feel lonely and left without, I will remember that misery has temporarily skewed my perception of reality, that I cannot see the whole story from where I stand, and that I do not serve a graceless, compassionless, or merciless God.

## REFLECTIONS FOR PERSONAL APPLICATION

1. Describe how you're feeling today. Did any words or phrases in this chapter resonate with your experience?
2. Note one insight you gleaned in this chapter about your experience of loneliness.
3. How would you describe your perception of God's disposition toward and dealings with you right now?
4. Why do you think it sometimes feels like God's mercies are for everyone but us?

# 8

# HOPE

## *A Call to Keep Going*

If I asked you, "How much longer will you feel so miserable?" your answer probably wouldn't be "Just another hour or two. Nearly done now!" Depression doesn't work that way. From our perspective, it may seem like our clock will be stuck at midnight forever. Well-intentioned platitudes, pep talks, or positive thoughts lose their effectiveness in this kind of misery. It hurts me to remember how awful it was to feel that way for so long. To sit in the pit of inexplicable misery, grieving the loss of the hope I once had.

### LOOKING FOR SIGNS OF LIFE

Returning to my room after the group session, I made what felt like a last-ditch effort to seek God's face. I sat on my bed and opened my Bible, something I hadn't been able to bring myself to do for weeks. Only, I wasn't flipping through its pages to seek out comfort or counsel—I was searching for signs of life. Something to signal that God was near. I didn't know how to keep going without him.

Perhaps you chose to read this book because you've been searching for much of the same. If that is the case, I want you to know that, however feeble it feels, your attempt to seek God's face in the midst of despair is a courageous act of faith in itself. Yes—the wick may be smoldering, but your seeking proves it's not been snuffed out (Isa. 42:3). Yes—depression's dirge "suggests that the sovereign Lord has abandoned [you] and become inactive," but your seeking suggests that for him to do such a thing "goes against the grain of [your] most cherished beliefs."[1] Even in the thick of misery, you are seeking the face of your Father in heaven. That's not proof that you're out of your mind—it's evidence that Christ's Spirit dwells in you (1 Cor. 3:16).

## SUBMERGED IN DARKNESS

By grace though faith, the Spirit of Christ is most assuredly with us (Eph. 1:13). Yet sometimes we feel dropped by him rather than carried, forsaken rather than kept, devoured more than delivered, ignored more than heard, hurt more than helped, despised more than loved. At such times, we naturally default to framing reality by our own thoughts, assumptions, and emotions.[2] We may be tempted to draw wrong conclusions about God's heart based on the pain and confusion in ours. And the longer he seems silent and distant, the darker this journey often feels.

Do you ever feel like the darkness is your closest friend (Ps. 88:18)? When life is full of affliction and misfortune, when grief and hardship persist, when relief and healing remain just out of reach, when people misunderstand and mishandle us, when we feel bereft and bankrupt, and when God seems to hide every time we groan for his help (Ps. 10:1; 22:1), darkness can offer itself as a refuge—a cave to curl up and hide in. Its shadows embrace us without so much as a word. They understand that we want to disappear or die.

These shadows do not nourish life, embolden courage, or strengthen our will. The darkness is not a refuge that revives. Deep down our souls sense this. We *know* we are "children of the light and of the day; we don't belong to darkness and night" (1 Thess. 5:5). But even so, here we are. We don't to want to hurt anymore.

We do not belong to darkness, yet we are surrounded by it.

## WEEPING FOR HIM

Charles Spurgeon tells us that "the iron bolt which so mysteriously fastens the door of hope and holds our spirits in gloomy prison, needs a heavenly hand to push it back."[3] When we arrive at this miserable place, we need Someone to come and rescue us—Someone with willing hands and a heart for setting captives free (Isa. 42:7; Luke 4:18; John 20:27; Rev. 1:18). We need a Person who is powerful enough—*merciful* enough—to bring light to our deadening darkness (Luke 1:78–79).

We need that heavenly hand. When will it come?

Maybe you're tired of crying to God for his help. Maybe you're not looking for his comfort or counsel. You're simply searching—groaning—for *him*, just like I was that day (Ps. 73:25). "Lord, please! I need you here with me. I don't know how to keep going without you!"

This desperate groan sounds like that of a child who is crying for her parent to come. If you've ever heard this plea in a moment of injury or distress, you know just how gut-wrenching it can be. The child isn't begging for an outcome—all she wants is for mom to be near. So we go to them as quick as we can. Somehow our closeness enables their endurance.

Likewise, "as a mother is tenderest to the most diseased and weakest child, so does Christ most mercifully incline to the weakest."[4] As we cry out not for outcomes but for *him*, Jesus cannot help but be stirred into action (Ps. 73:25; Isa. 63:9). It's the Lord's closeness that enables us to endure affliction. We need him to come down to us, cup our cheeks in his hands, and look us straight in the eyes.

We need to hear him say, "I'm committed to you. We'll go into the future together" (Deut. 31:8).

## MERCY

Reclining on my hospital bed that hot midafternoon, I listlessly thumbed through the book of Psalms. The promises that had formerly encouraged me seemed detached from the misery at hand. That my Bible could seem dead and dry only added to my grief.

My spirit was utterly broken that week in August. But one bittersweet day, as I sat locked within the confines of a psychiatric facility, the silence finally broke as well. I had been seen—I had been heard. Life sprang forth from a page that read me like a book:

> You are my strength; I wait for you to rescue me,
> for you, O God, are my fortress.
> In his unfailing love, my God will stand with me.
> He will let me look down in triumph on all my enemies. (Ps. 59:9–10)

I read, I gasped, and then I wept.

The Light—the Life—I had so desperately longed to see had come down to me. Through these hope-filled words, the Lord spoke to my soul in his still, small voice: "I am your strength and refuge. I love you. I stand with you. I'll raise you. You'll see."

## THE REFUGE

When you are in a prison, you need a *Person* to come to your rescue. So when God spoke to me through the words of Psalm 59, it was as if his hand had unlocked the iron bolt to the door. Suddenly, I dared to hope again. I dared to believe that if I watched for my Lord to meet me where I stood, he would. Not even the concrete walls of the hospital would keep him from coming down to me. All I had to do was wait and watch.

I had nowhere else to go and nothing to lose (John 6:68).

Stepping over to the window, I scanned the sprawling oak tree centered in the courtyard. But there were no creatures to look at—no fluttering butterflies or bouncing birds or marching ants. Nothing teemed with the vigor of life.

I put on my glasses and looked again.

Able to see through the window more clearly, I quickly noticed a squirrel on a tree branch—sleeping. *Sleeping!* Have you ever seen a squirrel fast asleep in the wild? I hadn't. They always seem to be in a hurry, constantly foraging and scurrying about. But this squirrel was different. In the heat of the day—the very time you'd expect her to be working—she had recognized her need for rest and come to the oak tree for refuge.

Instantly, I knew what it meant—as if the scene was staged just for me.

## INVITED TO REST

As I watched the squirrel, I realized how squirrel-like I had been in my constant striving. Like a hurried, busy-bodied creature, I had been working hard to "be fine" when hurts and heartbreak came. To me, suffering well meant being impervious to stress and sadness, as if questions and confusion weren't allowed. But my quest to achieve emotional stability left me hopelessly desperate. I wasn't seeing the fruits I thought faith would produce.

And yet, as I looked at the squirrel asleep in the tree, a fresh calmness quieted my soul. I saw how she trusted its shade for protection. She relied on its strength for stability. Knowing the tree would provide the cover she needed, she closed her eyes and napped in peace. There was no hurry or worry about her. The tree was hospitable. Life-giving.

I thought back to Psalm 59 and what it meant for the Lord to be "my fortress." I considered what it would look like to rest in him when the heat of life's troubles beat down upon me—to trust the shade of his shadow for protection, to rely on his strength and stability instead of striving for my own. My "fix-it" mindset had broken my spirit, but God in his unfailing love met me. He stepped down into my darkness to save me from myself.

In the solitude of my hospital room, I took my next step and entered his rest.

## A TREE OF HOPE

That week, the Lord showed me how to live in the midnight hour. I learned that depression wasn't an affliction to work myself out of but to walk with God through. And *when* I felt hopeless, weary, sad, angry, anxious, shamed, or lonely (or some muddled combination of the entire lot), I was to take refuge in the Lord (2 Sam. 22:3). Like the squirrel sleeping safely on the tree branch, I was to take my rest in the everlasting arms (Deut. 33:27).

Although the serenity of a squirrel napping in a tree is a hope-filled illustration for us to consider, it also prompts us to remember the mercy that lay in a very different set of branches—ones with a tattered body nailed to them. At the very center of our life stands the rugged cross of our crucified Savior. This tree was not hospitable but hostile. Not life-giving but life-taking.

Yet knowing that this tree—his cross—would become a beacon of hope to a broken people living in a broken world, Jesus was willing to step into our place and die the death we deserved. He saved us from eternal wrath. He delivered us from eternal sorrow. Surely the darkest day in all of history is where we get the brightest view of God's unfailing love—because to see Jesus at the apex of his misery is to perceive his mercy more clearly in our own.

He was despised and rejected—
    a man of sorrows, acquainted with deepest grief.
We turned our backs on him and looked the other way.
    He was despised, and we did not care.

Yet it was our weaknesses he carried;
    it was our sorrows that weighed him down.
And we thought his troubles were a punishment from God,
    a punishment for his own sins!
But he was pierced for our rebellion,
    crushed for our sins.
He was beaten so we could be whole.
    He was whipped so we could be healed. (Isa. 53:3–5)

Our Shepherd's voluntary sacrifice proves his devotion to his sheep (John 10:11). When we measure his unfailing love by the wood of the cross—not by our hurts or hardships or heartbreak—we see that he is sovereign *and* gracious, omnipotent *and* compassionate, just *and* merciful toward us (Deut. 32:4; Ps. 25:10). Because Christ finished his atoning work on the cross, we can rest safely in the shadow of his refuge (Ps. 57:1; John 19:30; Rom. 5:10).

Since through Christ we have peace with God, we can be at rest.

## GOD TAILORS HIS CARE

Although the cross proves God's concern for those who "live in a land of deep darkness" (Isa. 9:2), it's often hard to sense God's mercy when we feel stuck in depression. As we've seen in this book, sorrowful sufferers like us can struggle to perceive his loving hand as it works mysteriously and redemptively in our lives.

But we've also seen that God tailors his care to individuals and their particular experiences. The way he helped Moses was much different from how he helped Elijah. He wanted Gideon to "Go!"

but the bleeding woman to "Come!" And although he comforted Mary and Martha in their grief, he confronted Job in his. Yet he didn't misunderstand or mishandle any—he helped them all to take a step through the darkness (2 Cor. 1:3–4).

But what about Naomi? Were God's midnight mercies for her just as much as the others? Though her story doesn't include miraculous signs and wonders, Jehovah Jireh ("the God who provides") did supply everything she needed to turn the page and persevere. Though Naomi didn't experience a divine encounter, the Father of mercies commissioned a devoted companion (Ruth) and a kinsman-redeemer (Boaz) to serve as active agents of his love. And when these two agents married and bore a son, the women who once stared at Naomi in shock looked at her in joyful awe (Ruth 4:13–14). Not only had she been given a friend in Ruth and a family through Boaz, but in baby Obed she'd been given a future—a son she could set her hope on again (Ruth 4:17).

## GOD'S MERCIES ARE FOR YOU

That afternoon, it was as if the heavenly hand had picked the lock to my prison. All at once, I could set my hope on the Son again (1 Peter 1:13). His light was a candle in my darkness.

Nothing about my story had changed. And yet the Spirit had given me a fresh encounter with Jesus through his Word and world. I met him at the tree, saw how devoted he'd been to me, and under his easy yoke I took my rest (Ps. 116:7; Matt. 11:28). After my years of striving to be emotionally stable, Jesus clarified *his* goal for my life. I was to live for his glory. I was to take feeble steps of faith—one by one—while entrusting myself to him.

Perhaps today you find yourself feeling devastated by grief and loss. Maybe you're disheartened because the outcomes you've hoped for haven't come to fruition, or you're discouraged because you don't know why you feel depressed in the first place. When we don't understand God's upside-down ways or see the fruits we thought our faith would produce, it can lead us to conclude that God is against us. We may think he's finally given up on us—this time, for good.

Yet Naomi's story invites us to take notice of the gifts of grace we *have* been given to help us through this midnight hour. Maybe we don't have the story we want, but even as we lament our sorrow and disappointment, we can come to trust that God has given us everything we need to persevere through the story we're in (Rom. 8:32; 2 Peter 1:3):

- In Christ, we've been given a devoted Friend (and Kinsman-Redeemer) who fully knows, understands, and loves us no matter how badly we struggle with depression (Heb. 4:15).
- Through Christ, we belong to a family of believers—Spirit-filled people we can lean on for practical help, comfort, and counsel (Gal. 6:2; 1 Cor. 12:25; Heb. 12:1).
- Because of Christ, we have a bright and glorious future—one well-worth straining toward in the strength and power that God supplies (1 Cor. 2:9; Phil. 3:13–14; James 1:12).

A friend, a family, and a future. These gifts of grace are some of the means by which God nourishes life, emboldens courage, and strengthens wavering wills. And as the Holy Spirit works through his Word and world, we learn how to "take hold of the hope set before us" (Heb. 6:18 NIV)—how to rest in a love that will never let us go (Rom. 8:38–39).

## HOPE

The realistic hope Christ offers you today is not of this world. It's not groundless superstition or flimsy sentimentality—it neither promises nor produces a sorrow-free life. Rather, the hope Christ gives us is "an assured expectation that everything God has promised will come to pass."[5] And since the resurrection of Jesus proved these promises true—since "all of God's promises have been fulfilled in Christ with a resounding 'Yes!'" (2 Cor. 1:20)—we can set our hope fully on him and the grace that is to come (1 Tim. 4:10; 1 Peter 1:13).

The hope of a sorrow-free future is meant to help us brave a sorrow-full today (Rev. 21:4).

Ed Welch writes, "Hope is both a gift from God and a skill he enables us to attain."[6] This realization was a revelation for me. Knowing that I could learn how to faithfully express both hope and sorrow in a way that gives due weight to both was precisely the grace I needed for spiritual growth. No more pretending to be fine. No more despairing that I was stuck in depression.

Despite how it might seem today, in Christ you are God's *beloved* child. That means you needn't be a "better" child before you can be fully loved by your Father. You needn't pretend you're feeling happier than you are, just as you needn't despair because you're walking through this darkness. The hope God has given you in Christ is both a gift to receive and a skill to develop. You don't have to sense it to possess and practice it! Cry out to God and lament your dark days while trusting that they are numbered. Midnight is here but morning *must* come.

Depression we feel, but God we trust.

## OUR HIGHER PERSPECTIVE

To grieve with hope doesn't mean we'll grieve with ease. Rather, it means keeping our eternal inheritance in view as we lament our present sorrows (1 Peter 1:3–4). Because "we are citizens of heaven, where the Lord Jesus Christ lives" (Phil. 3:20), we have access to a higher perspective from which to interpret the temporary troubles we face (2 Cor. 4:17). This broken world is not our home. This one mortal life is not all the life we get (John

5:24). Someday soon, our joyous voices will roar with the angels on the final judgment day, when death, crying, sorrow, and pain finally pass away (Rev. 21:4). Sister, all our groans of misery will soon become roars of victory (Rom. 8:36–37). You will not hurt forever. In light of that unparalleled promise, we take hold of our hope and take heart.

Christ the Victor has defeated the darkness. His bright shining glory is guiding us home (1 Cor. 15:51–56).

## WALKING THE HARD PATH

We may never figure out every contributing factor to our experiences of depression. The shroud of mystery may remain until that day we "see everything with perfect clarity" (1 Cor. 13:12). But we can know what it means for Jesus to faithfully walk us through this midnight, even without complete self-knowledge (2 Cor. 5:7). We can know that we're not the only ones who've gone down this long and lonely road. And, perhaps more important, we can know that while all mothers bear burdens, Christian mothers carry crosses (Matt. 16:24). The path we walk on as believers is difficult because the gate to life is narrow (Matt. 7:13–14). But by God's grace, this hard path is refining our faith, shaping us into women of conviction and character (Ps. 119:71; Rom. 5:3–4; Phil. 1:6). Shaping us into the likeness of Christ (2 Cor. 3:18).

As you continue on your journey, remember that God has made *you* an agent of his love. You can be a friend. You are someone's family. You've been entrusted with a God-given gift or a soul-strengthening comfort to share. No matter how weak and weary you feel, you are indispensable (1 Cor. 12:22). Though Jesus needs nothing from you, the body of Christ needs what he plans to give through you (Acts 17:25; Rom. 12:4–8). You've not been left without love to give—so keep going, and keep giving it. Just as those who have struggled before us have become conduits of God's comfort to us, so we can become the same to others who are hopelessly desperate (2 Cor. 1:3–4).

You've not been left without the gospel—it's a treasure you cannot lose (2 Cor. 4:6–7).

Sister, you have not been (nor will you be) left without what you need to turn the page in your story. Depression has not separated you from God's love in the least (Rom. 8:38). He's still standing with you—still holding your hand, still guiding you with his counsel and escorting you into glory (Ps. 73:23–24). Yes, you have grief and hardship now, but you also have Christ's hands and his heart. Though you have fallen, you will surely rise, because *Jesus* is your light and your life (Micah 7:8; Rom. 8:11; Col. 3:4).

## NEXT STEP

Cease striving and rest yourself in the everlasting arms.

*And I will lead the blind*
*in a way that they do not know,*
*in paths that they have not known*
*I will guide them.*
*I will turn the darkness before them into light,*
*the rough places into level ground.*
*These are the things I do,*
*and I do not forsake them. (Isa. 42:16 ESV)*

## REMEMBER

When I feel like God's mercy is for everyone but me, I will look to the misery of Christ and remember that he knows the pain I feel, he sympathizes with my weaknesses, and he will not fail to bring me through, out, and up from the darkness—just as he promised.

## REFLECTIONS FOR PERSONAL APPLICATION

1. List words or phrases in this chapter that help you to describe how you're feeling today.
2. List one meaningful insight you gleaned in this chapter about your experience of depression.
3. List one step you can take today to apply what you've learned in this chapter to your situation.
4. List what you have learned about the mercy of God toward those who feel depressed today.

# EPILOGUE

Charles Spurgeon once preached, "Depression of spirit is no index of declining grace; the very loss of joy and the absence of assurance may be accompanied by the greatest advancement in the spiritual life."[1] This statement rings true to my experience—particularly in the weeks, months, and years following my psychiatric hospitalization and disorder diagnosis. That awful week was a major turning point for me because it was there that my heart became cemented in two truths:

1. There is zero hope for me in myself.
2. There is absolute hope for me in Jesus Christ.

How did God accomplish this supernatural work? Because I was experiencing immense cognitive difficulties, I struggled to read the Bible, let alone connect some of the dots between God's Word and my acute emotional distress (and I had some biblical counseling training, no less!). But in my weakness, the Lord mercifully strengthened me. He cleared my foggy mind long enough to read the works of Spirit-filled writers such as Ed Welch, Charles Hodges, Zack Eswine, and Charles Spurgeon, and they ministered God's Word to my despondent heart. Each helped me to frame what I was experiencing through a biblical lens and with biblical language. And although I didn't walk out of that hospital with pep in my step, I left certain that Jesus would enable me to turn the page and persevere—whatever came next.

I could learn to set my hope in God again, and that was a start.

The Lord was gentle and gracious with me as I came out of the worst depressive episode I'd ever experienced. He gave me a renewed sense of purpose. He provided me with creative outlets to channel my energy. He gave me the support of friends, loved ones, and a faithful church family to fellowship with. But after a period of restoration and healing, we entered into four years of nonstop trials and loss. An autoimmune disease struck down our daughter, severely debilitating her body while shrouding her heart and mind in despair; the stillbirth of our first nephew, Timothy, slammed our whole family down with grief; a global pandemic locked down the world and took down old friends; a sudden house fire turned our lives upside-down in a matter of minutes; and private parenting problems left my husband and me feeling weighed down and betrayed.

I share this because even though I'm no longer being treated for depression or bipolar disorder II, I don't want to give the impression that I've arrived at some sort of emotional or spiritual pinnacle. These trials and losses were excruciating, and we did not navigate them sinlessly. Half of them occurred while I was trying to write this book, and all of them were unexpected and entirely beyond our abilities to fix, control, or understand. We cried and mourned and lamented and argued and reasoned and confessed and repented and prayed and reconciled on a seemingly never-ending loop. Some days were so hard and dark that all we could do was sit in the pain and watch life break before our eyes.

"But as a result, we stopped relying on ourselves and learned to rely only on God, who raises the dead" (2 Cor. 1:9).

After nearly fifteen years of cyclical emotional turmoil, this absolute conviction of hopelessness in self was a great advancement in my spiritual life. And with each passing trial and tragedy, I more quickly yielded to the mysteries of God's good providence. Yes, our circumstances were distressing, but they became occasions for me to turn and talk to God—to practice pouring out my heart, repenting of my sin, asking for his help, refusing false refuges, accepting his will, and taking hold of the hope he set before me. I learned to wait for God's plans to unfurl while focusing my energy and attention on the responsibilities before me, constantly turning to friends for prayer, counsel, and encouragement. And over and over again this Spirit-empowered process continued.

Over and over he continues this work in me still.

So, while I pray that God would use this book to comfort and counsel you, I've avoided offering a cookie-cutter, faith-informed formula by which you can endure your trials without sorrow or sin. That's an unrealistic goal. Instead, I hope to have helped you to connect some of the dots between God's Word and your acute emotional distress—to frame what you're experiencing through a biblical lens and with biblical language. No, maybe you won't walk away from our time together with pep in your step, but perhaps you're becoming increasingly certain that Jesus will enable you to turn the page and persevere. And if all you get from this book is a fresh sense that you can set your hope in God again, that's not merely a start.

It's the beginning of a great advancement.

# ACKNOWLEDGMENTS

To me, this book is a miracle. Maybe that sounds dramatic, but I cannot even begin to describe how impossible this project seemed at times or how many hardships took place as I tried to write it. I am convinced that you hold *Midnight Mercies* in your hands today because of a great many prayers offered by a great many people. That, and because of God's unmerited kindness to me, which I experienced so intimately and richly as I stumbled through this journey. Thank you, Abba Father, for bringing me to yourself and calling me your daughter. This book is more than a sacrifice of praise—it's a declaration of your perfect love for me and my imperfect yet earnest love for you.

Although the influences of a number of Christian brothers and sisters seep through the sentences in this book, there are some whose friendship and ministry have been particularly invaluable to me. With respect to the arduous journey of writing this book, I thank God for Shannon McCoy, Paul Tautges, Sarah Walton, Dave Almack, Amanda Martin, and the entire P&R Publishing team. I only made it to the finish line because of God's grace given through each of you.

Thank you, Pam MacDowell, for your faithful weekly check-ins and prayers not only for this project but for my family and for my walk with Christ. And thank you, Ann Kroeker, for patiently coaching me after our house fire when I couldn't think straight, let alone write.

I am also grateful to all of my co-laborers in the gospel at the Institute for Biblical Counseling & Discipleship (IBCD), as well as the church families who have walked with our family in both good and sad times: Covenant Grace Church, Grace Church, Trinity Point Church, and Covenant Presbyterian Church.

To the Christian brothers whose books went with me to the mental hospital, I dare not try to imagine what might have become of my life if it weren't for the Spirit working through your writing ministry that week. Thank you to Edward Welch, Zack Eswine, Charles Hodges, and Charles Spurgeon for allowing God to work through your gifts of teaching and communication.

In an effort to keep myself from writing a mini-book's worth of acknowledgments, which I'm sure I could easily do, I'd also like to publicly thank the following brothers and sisters: Nancy Albao, Jon Bloom, Barbra Burgess, Amy and Eddie Campbell, Erick and Natasha Cobb, Sabo and Beth Cortez, John and Amy Creel, Mike Emlet, Elyse Fitzpatrick, Rebecca Fort, Greg and Cheryl Goodnight, Robert and Ann Maree Goudzwaard, Chad and Ashley Hall, Mary Harlow, Megan Hill, Ana Jackson, Dave Jenkins, Kenny and Debra Keahey, Timothy Keller, Kelly Lattimer, Jim and Caroline Newheiser, Christina Nunez, John Piper, David Powlison, Tony Reinke, Chris and Kimi Sturgess, Paul David Tripp, Mark Vroegop, Aimee White, and Rush Witt.

Lastly, I thank God for my family. Thank you to my brothers, Tim and Kevin, and to my in-laws for your love and support. Thank you to my mother, Diane, for being my most devoted cheerleader, and to my late father, Timothy, for being a safe and steady presence in an unsafe and unsteady world. Thanks also to "Mr. Tim" Sarazen for loving my mom, my brothers, and me so well since Dad's death. To my baby birds, Brianna, Cash, and Charlotte—Mommy loves you always and so very, very much. And to my husband, Brett, whose sacrifice of time and resources enabled this project to finally come to fruition: thank you for being strong where I am weak. May God keep strengthening our love for his glory.

*Appendix A*

# WHEN GRIEF BECOMES DANGEROUS—AND WHAT TO DO ABOUT IT

Medical doctor and biblical counselor Charles Hodges writes, "It is no accident that when we suffer loss, we respond emotionally for a time and with an intensity that matches the problem. God made us that way in his image."[1] In one sense, this reality is comforting. We know from Scripture that anguished tears can be a faithful response to loss,[2] and it is normal for us to experience sadness—"for a variety of identifiable reasons"[3]—until Christ sees fit to return or call us home (Rev. 21:4).

But perhaps Hodges's statement also leaves you wondering about the time and intensity of your grief. If your sadness feels too strong for too long, does that mean grief has morphed into depression?

This is a complex question to answer. Growing through grief is not formulaic. And while suffering loss is a universal human experience, it is also an intensely personal one that no two people encounter, interpret, and process exactly alike. Intense and prolonged grief isn't necessarily tied to clinical depression, just as intense and prolonged depression isn't necessarily tied to loss-related grief. It's not wise to make absolute statements in either direction. We overlook the individuality of the sufferer and the painful specifics of her story when we do.

For these reasons, I like to approach this question in a way other than rehearsing a list of subjective symptoms and timeframes. I've found that instead of trying to draw a line between my griefs and my experiences of depression (as if they could always be so neatly separated!), I've been more helped by considering when sadness is *safe* and when it becomes *dangerous.* This has given me a gracious amount of room to feel and process my sorrows with God while still acknowledging that there are occasions when loss-related sadness becomes concerning.

## WHEN IS OUR SADNESS SAFE?

So how might we gauge whether the sadness we are experiencing today is safe or dangerous? Let's start by considering what comes to mind when we think of safety. For me, the word *safe* stirs up childhood memories of playing tag and touching "base" (usually a tree) to avoid being tagged "it." Every player knew that base was a safe place to be—somewhere we could stop, catch our breath, and rest without the fear of being tagged. In other words, base was regarded by all as a real and present refuge from danger.

The same is true of the kind of sadness that is safe. When our grief leads us to take refuge in Christ—when it compels us to rest "beneath the shadow of [his] wings until the danger passes by" (Ps. 57:1)—it promotes healing. In this way, sadness can be safe (productive, even) because it drives us "to the only place and power that bring about real change"[4] in our lives. Yes, we cry anguished tears and lament. We wrestle with fears and reel from pain. But sadness is safe when it propels us to bring our hurt and heartbreak to the Lord, that we might come to rest in the everlasting arms (Deut. 33:27).

"Keep me safe, my God," David laments, "for in you I take refuge" (Ps. 16:1 NIV).

## WHEN IS OUR SADNESS DANGEROUS?

Do you know what it is like for confusion and pain to persist while your sorrows loom large over the rest of life? If so, you know how hard it can sometimes be for our souls to be comforted. We need to acknowledge that some losses are so painful—some memories are so terrible—that they remain inconsolable this side of heaven. As pastor and author Zach Eswine observes, "Even if we are wise and knowledgeable by [God's] grace, there are still things and seasons in our lives that we 'cannot bear . . . now' (John 16:12)."[5]

For us to cry over inconsolable things does not mean that our grief is unfaithful.

Having said that, we also need to acknowledge that sometimes when we cannot bear our grief, we may struggle to sense that we are safely held by God. Instead, we may feel as though he is handling us harshly. We may doubt his goodness and question his wisdom. We may feel angry about what's happened and afraid of what comes next. These are all normal responses to loss—ones which God invites us to process *with* him through lament. (I've written more about this in appendix B.)

But while our groans over inconsolable things may lead us to honest cries of faith, sometimes they signal a dire disconnect between what we *know* to be true and what we *feel* to be true about God and his promises. This disconnect can leave us feeling disoriented—disillusioned, even. And when God does not immediately clarify our confusion, remedy our grief, lift our darkness, or alleviate our pain, we may grow hopelessly desperate and try to take relief into our own hands.

The night before my hospitalization, Jesus appeared to be absent. I had been crying for his help for weeks, seemingly to no avail. I was confused by his silence, surprised by the depths of my grief, and hurt by what I interpreted to be his indifference to my pain. I felt harshly handled—*not* safely held. As a result, I took grief relief into my own hands by way of alcohol and self-harm. From the perspective of my hopeless desperation, darkness seemed much preferable to light (Ps. 88:18).[6]

Sadness can become dangerous when Jesus does not seem to be a real refuge to run to.

## IMMEDIATE HELP FOR DANGEROUS SADNESS

Dangerous sadness is concerning at any stage of grief, particularly when it drives us to seek rest and relief through substances, self-harm, or self-destructive habits. In saying this, I am *not* condemning those whose grief has taken a turn toward the danger zone. I'm not saying if these people only had more faith, then they wouldn't be struggling so severely with their grief. All of us are prone to seek rest and refuge apart from Christ, especially when life hurts. How much more difficult is it, then, when we've tried to turn to him but he seems absent or indifferent?

By distinguishing between safe and dangerous sadness, we can better determine what kind of care and counsel will be most beneficial to us. This allows us to take next steps that address our spiritual, physical, and practical needs for a particular season. And, perhaps most urgently, this allows us to devise responsible, God-honoring plans to get our broken hearts to a place where we can take the time to process our sorrows safely.

If you find yourself struggling with dangerous sadness today—if you cannot perceive that Christ is a real and trustworthy refuge for you to rest in—I want you to know two truths. First, you are not the only person—not the only mother—whose desperation for relief from grief has driven her to self-medicate in some way. I hope that by sharing this part of my story, you sense my sympathy.

This *is* hard. You *are* suffering. But there are life-sustaining steps you can take in the coming days and weeks that will help you to navigate the ongoing pain of your grief wisely. Here are a few of the steps that have been most helpful to me:

1. **Describe your "felt reality."** What does it feel like to be living with grief today? How you answer that question describes your *felt reality*—a perspective that is framed by your own thoughts, assumptions, and emotions.[7] Using the lyrics found in Psalm 88, make a list of words or phrases that help you to honestly articulate your current frame of mind.
2. **Lament your "felt reality."** Using the list you created, cry out to God in prayer and tell him what you are feeling and thinking right now—even if you aren't sure if he's listening or if it will make a difference in how you feel. Engage the Lord by asking him questions. Give voice to your complaint. Submit what you *feel* to be true about God to what you *know* to be true about him, according to his Word.
3. **Ask God to show you how to live, even as you grieve.** When it comes to walking through grief, feeble steps of faith are acts of courage. Ask God to show you how to take your next small, life-sustaining step forward, according to the moment you're in. Trust that you are *already* safely at "base" because you belong to Jesus. He's holding your hand, guiding you with his counsel, and leading you heavenward day by day (Ps. 73:23–24).
4. **Build a support team.** Proverbs 11:14 says, "In an abundance of counselors there is safety" (ESV). Ask your husband, a family member, or a friend for help to assemble a group of people who can care for you during this time. This group may include mature believers, counselors, advocates, nutritionists, social workers, pastors or elders, medical doctors, or other

professionals who can offer the interventions and resources needed to bring you back to a place of stability.

5. **Resist taking relief into your own hands.** In my case, this meant establishing an immediate (and subsequently lifelong) prohibition of alcohol. This was one step I could immediately take for the sake of my health and healing. If *you* regularly turn to particular substances, self-harm behaviors, or self-destructive habits when seeking rest or relief from emotional pain, confess these tendencies to your support team and ask for their help in making practical changes or establishing safeguards in this area.

Sister, God does not expect us to suffer sorrow stoically, but he does want us to learn how to grieve safely and with hope. If today you feel blinded by loss and all the pain and confusion that comes with it, tell him so. Your prayers of lament are not useless exercises but sustaining graces that will get you through the day. And while you wouldn't have chosen these inconsolable griefs for yourself, you can choose today how you're going to respond when future sorrows swell. With the support of your team and a plan of action, you can take your next step in the strength God supplies.

Wait and watch for Jesus, sister. He's redeeming your grief to grow you in his grace.

# *Appendix B*

# PRAYERS OF LAMENT IN DEPRESSION

If there's one thing I wish I'd known before my hospitalization, it is the language of biblical lament. Sure, I was familiar with the Psalms. I resonated deeply with the psalmists' frequent cries of distress and despair. But I didn't really understand the intentional nature of lament and why God invites us to use it. I just knew that the Psalms put words to my pain on days when it felt like I couldn't.

However, after reading Mark Vroegop's book *Dark Clouds, Deep Mercy*, I discovered that biblical lament is one means by which we can practice the skill of hope as we walk through depression—particularly because it helps us to process emotional pain in a safe and productive way. Whether or not you are familiar with biblical lament, this resource is meant to give you some basic insight and a practical structure you can start using today.

## TAKING REFUGE IN JESUS THROUGH LAMENT

In his helpful book, Vroegop highlights four common components of biblical lament that are easily observed in the Psalms. To make these four components easier for you to remember, I slightly adjusted the wording in order to construct an acronym: EVAC. *Evac*uate—move from danger to safety—by approaching Jesus in your distress through lament.

**E**ngage your God
**V**oice your complaint
**A**sk for help
**C**ommit to trust

The acronym above not only helps to reinforce the concept of taking refuge in Jesus through prayer but also to guide us through each of lament's equally important components. Ultimately, this biblically derived pattern gives us the grace to talk to God about our pain while guiding us to entrust it to him. And that's where the Lord wants lament to lead us—to a deeper conviction that he can be trusted despite what we think, what we feel, or what we see around us.

## PRACTICING LAMENT IN DEPRESSION

Knowing these four basic components helps to clarify what lament is (and isn't), but perhaps you need more direction to practice *evac*uating to Jesus in this way. First, it will be helpful to see lament in action by reading the laments that God's people have sung throughout history. My favorite psalms of lament are Psalms 6, 13, 22, 31, 32, 38, 42, 55, 69, 73, 77, 88, and 102. Though there are many more, these have repeatedly ministered to me on my darkest days, so I commend them to you. As you read these psalms, see if you can locate components of a safe *evac*uation.

Second, although there are no exact "formulas" for biblical lament, the following prompts can help you to get started. Give lament a try by completing the sentences below:

- Lord, today I feel like . . .
- I feel this way because . . .
- My complaint is that . . .
- I want to know . . .
- God, according to your Word, I'm asking you to . . .
- Show me how to live with this pain, because right now I feel like . . .
- But I know that you are . . .
- You promise to . . .
- Lord, I am choosing to trust you with . . .
- Please help my heart to rest as I wait for your will to unfold. In Jesus's name, amen.

Let's look at an example.

> Lord, today I feel like I'm never going to change. I feel this way because every time I think I'm doing better, life seems to get dark again. My complaint is that it doesn't seem like you're helping me at all. I want to know why you won't free me from the prison of depression after all the times I've asked you to.
>
> God, according to your Word, I'm asking you to bring light to my darkness—help me to endure my sorrow while I wait on you for help. Show me how to live with this pain, because right now I feel like I won't survive it.
>
> Jesus, I know that you are good, you are near, and you know just what this misery is like. You promise to never leave me or forsake me, and you promise to bear me up, day by day.
>
> Lord, I'm committing to trust you with my depression. Please help my heart to rest as I wait for your will to unfold. In Jesus's name, amen.

Take a close look at what you've written based on the psalms you've read and the prompts you've followed. You've said some hard things in this prayer, haven't you? You've honestly expressed your pain and openly aired your complaints. You've recalled God's promises and boldly asked him to act on them. But notice that you've also shifted. You've begun to rehearse what you know to be true about Jesus. You've counseled your soul to stand on his promise like the rock-solid foundation it is, and you've reaffirmed your commitment to trust in Christ even as you wrestle with fears and doubts.

That's faith, sister. And it's beautiful.

## I LAMENTED . . . NOW WHAT?

As you know, lament doesn't offer immediate grief relief. God has asked us to wait and watch for his plan to unfold as he carries us into tomorrow. Yet the tension of unresolved pain may still leave us feeling anxious to do something—*anything*—to calm our inner turmoil. Thankfully, God gives us something to do while we wait: love him with all our hearts and strength and love our neighbors as ourselves.

Look around. What responsibilities has God given to you? Surrender your concerns about the future to him while walking forward in those responsibilities today. Who has God put in your path or on your mind to love—a spouse, child, friend, or total stranger? Put off fruitless self-focus and put on service to others. And on the days when you feel so weary that you haven't the strength to be physically active, remember God's merciful care for Elijah and receive the grace of life-sustaining basics.

Pray. Eat. Drink. Sleep. Some days this is what courageous dependence on Jesus looks like.

Will you feel better after all this? My guess is probably not. But remember, that's not the point of lament. It's not meant to be an immediate "feel better" formula but a faith-building language that sustains us in sorrow. With the Holy Spirit's help, and a little bit of practice, you can learn to speak these prayers more frequently and fluently. God has given us this prayer instruction in his Word—he invites us to cry out to him in this way! So practice the skill of hope through lament. It's a step in the right direction.

# NOTES

## Introduction: Starting Our Journey

1. Kristen Fuller, "The Dangers of Mommy Needs Wine: Alcohol and Motherhood," *Psychology Today*, January 24, 2021, https://www.psychologytoday.com/us/blog/happiness-is-state-mind/202101/the-dangers-mommy-needs-wine-alcohol-and-motherhood.

## Chapter 1: Hopelessness

1. My father died of cancer when I was twenty-eight, but the Lord did not keep me fatherless for long. Two weeks after the death of my earthly father, Jesus guided me to my heavenly One—a midnight mercy I am eternally grateful for.
2. C. H. Spurgeon, *The Silent Shades of Sorrow: Healing for the Wounded* (Ross-shire, UK: Christian Focus, 2015), 33.
3. Gerard Van Groningen, "Numbers," in *Evangelical Commentary on the Bible*, Baker Reference Library (Grand Rapids: Baker Book House, 1995), 3:92.
4. Common ways we try to find rest apart from God include self-harm, excessive sleep, substances, shopping, video streaming services, or other destructive habits that temporarily disengage us from reality or attempt to numb our emotional pain.
5. Van Groningen, "Numbers," 3:92.
6. Drew Hunter, *Made for Friendship: The Relationship That Halves Our Sorrows and Doubles Our Joys* (Wheaton, IL: Crossway), 65.

## Chapter 2: Weariness

1. Zack Eswine, *Spurgeon's Sorrows: Realistic Hope for Those Who Suffer from Depression* (Ross-shire, UK: Christian Focus, 2014), 35.
2. C. H. Spurgeon, *The Silent Shades of Sorrow: Healing for the Wounded* (Ross-shire, UK: Christian Focus, 2015), 52.
3. Gerard Van Groningen, "1–2 Kings," in *Evangelical Commentary on the Bible*, vol. 3, Baker Reference Library (Grand Rapids: Baker Book House, 1995), 248.
4. Spurgeon, *Silent Shades of Sorrow*, 72.
5. *The Free Dictionary*, s.v. "supermom (*noun*)," accessed January 16, 2022, https://www.thefreedictionary.com/supermom.
6. Jen Oshman, *Enough about Me: Finding Lasting Joy in the Age of Self* (Wheaton, IL: Crossway, 2020), 27.
7. Fannie Lou Hamer, speech delivered at the Williams Institutional CME Church, Harlem, New York, December 20, 1964, available at https://www.crmvet.org/docs/flh64.htm.
8. Rush Witt, *I Want to Escape: Reaching for Hope When Life Is Too Much* (Greensboro, NC: New Growth Press, 2022), 7.
9. Kristy Etheridge, "Joni Eareckson Tada on Disability: 'God, if I Can't Die, Show Me How to Live,'" Billy Graham Evangelistic Association, September 8, 2014, https://billygraham.org/story/joni-eareckson-tada-on-disability-god-if-i-cant-die-show-me-how-to-live. Emphasis added.
10. Donald J. Wiseman, *1 and 2 Kings: An Introduction and Commentary*, Tyndale Old Testament Commentaries, vol. 9 (Downers Grove, IL: InterVarsity Press, 1993), 184.
11. Elijah's despair had temporarily blinded him to the good work God had accomplished in his life. The same can happen with us when we're sick and tired—we overlook the good work God has done in and through us, choosing instead to focus on our perceived failures, limitations, and disappointments.
12. The heart-probing questions I'm referring to can come through the ministry of God's Word through God's Spirit-filled people, our

personal engagement with the Scriptures, and sometimes even as the Spirit ministers to us while we behold the glory of God as revealed in the world he created.

## Chapter 3: Sadness

1. Daniel R. Berger II, *Rethinking Depression: Not a Sickness, Not a Sin* (Taylors, SC: Alethia International Ministries, 2019), 31.
2. John J. Bimson, "1 and 2 Kings," in *New Bible Commentary: 21st Century Edition*, ed. D. A. Carson et al., 4th ed. (Leicester, England; Downers Grove, IL: Inter-Varsity Press, 1994), 360.
3. Barclay Moon Newman and Eugene Albert Nida, *A Handbook on the Gospel of John*, UBS Handbook Series (New York: United Bible Societies, 1993), 365.
4. Tim Challies, *Seasons of Sorrow: The Pain of Loss and the Comfort of God* (Grand Rapids: Zondervan, 2022), 29.
5. Cameron Cole, *Therefore I Have Hope: 12 Truths that Comfort, Sustain, and Redeem in Tragedy* (Wheaton, IL: Crossway, 2018), 38–39.
6. I've loosely based this statement on the Latin phrases "Post tenebras lux" and "Post tenebras spero lucem," which translate to "After darkness . . . light" and "After darkness I hope for light," respectively.
7. Mark Vroegop, *Dark Clouds, Deep Mercy: Discovering the Grace of Lament* (Wheaton, IL: Crossway, 2019), 37.

## Chapter 4: Anger

1. Edward T. Welch, *Depression: A Stubborn Darkness* (Greensboro, NC: New Growth Press, 2004), 153.
2. J. Alasdair Groves and Winston T. Smith, *Untangling Emotions* (Wheaton, IL: Crossway, 2019), 170.
3. David Powlison, "Anger at God," *Journal of Biblical Counseling* 30, no. 2 (2016): 53.
4. William David Reyburn, *A Handbook on the Book of Job, UBS Handbook Series* (New York: United Bible Societies, 1992), 62.

5. Powlison, "Anger at God," 49–50.
6. Brad Hambrick, *Angry with God: An Honest Journey through Suffering and Betrayal* (Greensboro, NC: New Growth Press, 2022), 105.
7. Christopher Ash, *Job: The Wisdom of the Cross* (Wheaton, IL: Crossway, 2014), 319.
8. Ash, 208.
9. Ash, 376.
10. Frederick S. Leahy, *The Cross He Bore: Meditations on the Sufferings of the Redeemer* (Carlisle, PA: The Banner of Truth Trust, 2011), 26.

**Chapter 5: Anxiety**

1. The physiological impacts of anxiety are not the focus of this book. If anxiety has significantly impacted your routine daily functioning, it's wise to speak with your doctor to explore potential underlying contributing factors and practical steps you can take to alleviate some of the symptoms you are experiencing. Sometimes medical intervention can offer short-term help, but every person is different. What is beneficial for some may not be for others. For additional resources on anxiety and panic attacks, consult the recommended resource section in the appendix.
2. Pamela Gannon & Beverly Moore, *In the Aftermath: Past the Pain of Childhood Sexual Abuse* (Bemidji, MN: Focus Publishing, 2017), 77.
3. See Edward T. Welch, *I Have a Psychiatric Diagnosis: What Does the Bible Say?* (Greensboro, NC: New Growth Press, 2022), 24.
4. Daniel Isaac Block, *Judges, Ruth*, The New American Commentary (Nashville: Broadman & Holman Publishers, 1999), 260.
5. Paul David Tripp offers a helpful contrast between our concerns and responsibilities in his book, *Instruments in the Redeemer's Hands* (Phillipsburg, NJ: P&R Publishing, 2002), 252. In it, he defines concerns as "things that are important to a person, yet beyond [her] ability to bring about" and responsibilities as "things that God, in his word, calls [us] to do in [our] present situation and relationships."

6. Timothy Keller (@timkellernyc), "Worry is not believing God will get it right," July 13, 2018, https://twitter.com/timkellernyc/status/1017774149333323776.

## Chapter 6: Shame

1. John Bunyan, *Pilgrim's Progress* (Abbotsford, WI: Life Sentence Publishing, LLC, 2014) 88.
2. Edward T. Welch, *A Small Book about Why We Hide: How Jesus Rescues Us from Insecurity, Regret, Failure, and Shame* (Greensboro, NC: New Growth Press, 2021), 4.
3. See John D. Grassmick, "Mark," in *The Bible Knowledge Commentary: An Exposition of the Scriptures,* ed. J. F. Walvoord and R. B. Zuck, vol. 2 (Wheaton, IL: Victor Books, 1985), 125.
4. Ronald J. Kernaghan, *Mark,* The IVP New Testament Commentary Series (Downers Grove, IL: InterVarsity Press, 2007), 110.
5. Edward T. Welch, *Shame Interrupted: How God Lifts the Pain of Worthlessness and Rejection* (Greensboro, NC: New Growth Press, 2012), 134.
6. John D. Grassmick, "Mark," in *The Bible Knowledge Commentary: An Exposition of the Scriptures,* ed. J. F. Walvoord and R. B. Zuck (Wheaton, IL: Victor Books, 1985), 2:125.

## Chapter 7: Loneliness

1. Jayne V. Clark, "Loneliness: God's Remedy," *Journal of Biblical Counseling* 23, no. 4 (2005): 8.
2. Daniel Isaac Block, *Judges, Ruth,* vol. 6, *The New American Commentary* (Nashville: Broadman & Holman Publishers, 1999), 634.
3. Arthur E. Cundall and Leon Morris, *Judges and Ruth: An Introduction and Commentary,* vol. 7, Tyndale Old Testament Commentaries (Downers Grove, IL: InterVarsity Press, 1968), 247.
4. Block, *Judges, Ruth,* 645.
5. Cundall and Morris, *Judges and Ruth,* 253.
6. Block, *Judges, Ruth,* 647.

### Chapter 8: Hope


1. Biblical Studies Press, *The NET Bible First Edition Notes, Bible.org* (Richardson, TX: Biblical Studies Press, 2006), Ps. 77:10.
2. Joe Rigney, "Submit Your Felt Reality to God," Desiring God, May 19, 2022, https://www.desiringgod.org/articles/submit-your-felt-reality-to-god.
3. Charles H. Spurgeon, *Lectures to My Students* (Grand Rapids: Zondervan, 1972), 163. Quoted in John Piper, "Charles Spurgeon: Preaching through Adversity," Desiring God, January 31, 1995, https://www.desiringgod.org/messages/charles-spurgeon-preaching-through-adversity.
4. Richard Sibbes, *The Bruised Reed* (Edinburg, UK; The Banner of Truth Trust, 1998), 10.
5. John Crotts, *Hope: Living Confidently in God* (Phillipsburg, NJ; P&R Publishing, 2021).
6. Edward T. Welch, *Depression: A Stubborn Darkness* (Greensboro, NC: New Growth Press, 2004), 79.


### Epilogue


1. Charles Haddon Spurgeon, "Sweet Stimulants for the Fainting Soul," The Spurgeon Center, originally preached December 16, 1850, accessed October 14, 2022, https://www.spurgeon.org/resource-library/sermons/sweet-stimulants-for-the-fainting-soul.


### Appendix A: When Grief Becomes Dangerous—and What to Do about It


1. Charles Hodges, *Good Mood, Bad Mood: Help and Hope for Depression and Bipolar Disorder* (Wapwallopen, PA: Shepherd Press, 2012), 79.
2. As we see in passages such as Job 1:20, 22; Ecclesiastes 3:1, 4; and John 16:20.
3. Hodges, *Good Mood, Bad Mood*, 36.
4. Hodges, 89.

5. Zach Eswine, *Sensing Jesus: Life and Ministry as a Human Being* (Wheaton, IL: Crossway, 2013), 96.
6. If you are experiencing suicidal thoughts or urges to self-harm, please seek immediate help by reaching out to a trusted friend, family member, mentor, pastor, counselor, or local medical or emergency personnel, or by dialing the Suicide & Crisis Lifeline at 988 (for US Callers).
7. Joe Rigney, "Submit Your Felt Reality to God," Desiring God, May 19, 2022, https://www.desiringgod.org/articles/submit-your-felt-reality-to-god.

# RECOMMENDED READING

## FOR DEPRESSION


Chappell, Christine. *Help! I've Been Diagnosed with a Mental Disorder.* Wapwallopen, PA: Shepherd Press, 2021.

Emlet, Michael R. *Descriptions and Prescriptions: A Biblical Perspective on Psychiatric Diagnoses and Medications.* Greensboro, NC: New Growth Press, 2017.

Eswine, Zack. *Spurgeon's Sorrows: Realistic Hope for Those Who Suffer from Depression.* Scotland, UK: Christian Focus Publications Ltd., 2014.

Hodges, Charles D. *Good Mood Bad Mood: Hope and Help for Depression and Bipolar Disorder.* Wapwallopen, PA: Shepherd Press, 2013.

Lloyd-Jones, Martin D. *Spiritual Depression: Its Causes and Cure.* Grand Rapids: Wm. B. Eerdmans Publishing Company, 1965.

Welch, Edward T. *Blame It on the Brain? Distinguishing Chemical Imbalances, Brain Disorders, and Disobedience.* Phillipsburg, NJ: P&R Publishing, 1998.

———. *Depression: Looking Up from the Stubborn Darkness.* Greensboro, NC: New Growth Press, 2004.

———. *I Have a Psychiatric Diagnosis: What Does the Bible Say?* Greensboro, NC: New Growth Press, 2022.

## FOR GRIEF AND SUFFERING

Bridges, Jerry. *Trusting God: Even When Life Hurts*. Colorado Springs: NavPress, 1988.

Challies, Tim. *Seasons of Sorrow: The Pain of Loss and the Comfort of God*. Grand Rapids: Zondervan, 2022.

Cole, Cameron. *Therefore I Have Hope: 12 Truths that Sustain, Comfort, and Redeem in Tragedy*. Wheaton, IL: Crossway, 2018.

Guthrie, Nancy. *Hearing Jesus Speak into Your Sorrow*. Carol Stream, IL: Tyndale House Publishers, 2009.

Hambrick, Brad. *Angry with God: An Honest Journey through Suffering and Betrayal*. Greensboro, NC: New Growth Press, 2022.

Kellemen, Robert. *Grief: Walking with Jesus*. Phillipsburg, NJ: P&R Publishing, 2018.

Marshall, Glenna. *The Promise Is His Presence: Why God Is Always Enough*. Phillipsburg, NJ: P&R Publishing, 2019.

Smith, Esther. *Chronic Illness: Walking by Faith*. Phillipsburg, NJ: P&R Publishing, 2020.

Tautges, Paul. *A Small Book for the Hurting Heart: Meditations on Loss, Grief, and Healing*. Greensboro, NC: New Growth Press, 2020.

Vroegop, Mark. *Dark Clouds, Deep Mercy: Discovering the Grace of Lament*. Wheaton, IL: Crossway, 2019.

Weatherwell, Kristen and Sarah Walton. *Hope When It Hurts: Biblical Reflections to Help You Grasp God's Purpose in Your Suffering*. Epsom, UK: Good Book Company, 2017.

Whitman, Lauren. *A Painful Past: Healing and Moving Forward*. Phillipsburg, NJ: P&R Publishing, 2020.

## FOR EMOTIONS

Brownback, Lydia. *Finding God in My Loneliness*. Wheaton, IL: Crossway, 2017.

Crotts, John. *Hope: Living Confidently in God.* Phillipsburg, NJ: P&R Publishing, 2021.

Groves, J. Alasdair and Winston T. Smith. *Untangling Emotions.* Wheaton, IL: Crossway, 2019.

Hill, Megan. *Patience: Waiting with Hope.* Phillipsburg, NJ: P&R Publishing, 2021.

Jones, Robert. *Anger: Calming Your Heart.* Phillipsburg, NJ: P&R Publishing, 2019.

Liu, Esther. *Shame: Being Known and Loved.* Phillipsburg, NJ: P&R Publishing, 2019.

Tautges, Paul. *Anxiety: Knowing God's Peace.* Phillipsburg, NJ: P&R Publishing, 2019.

Wallace, Sara. *Created to Care: God's Truth for Anxious Moms.* Phillipsburg, NJ: P&R Publishing, 2019.

Did you find this book helpful?
Consider writing a review online.
We appreciate your feedback!

Or write to P&R at editorial@prpbooks.com
with your comments. We'd love to hear from you.